'Walk Humble,

Growing up in Ascott-under-Wychwood, 1918 – 1939

Eric R. Moss

including

My Personal Memories

Doris May Warner

❦

22/10/99

To ~: Mr Peter Barrell, With my best wishes for himself and family, always.
Sincerely
Eric R Moss

Eric and some of his brothers and sisters about 1925: (left to right, top to bottom) William and Ruth; Eric and Percy; Cyril and Vera.

'Walk Humble, My Son'

Growing up in Ascott-under-Wychwood, 1918–1939

by Eric R. Moss

Including
'My Personal Memories'
by Doris May Warner

The Wychwood Press

Published in 1999 by The Wychwood Press
— An imprint of Jon Carpenter Publishing —
2, The Spendlove Centre, Charlbury, Oxfordshire OX7 3PQ
Tel/fax 01608 811969

ISBN 1 902279 07 7

Printed in England by J. W. Arrowsmith Ltd., Bristol
Cover printed by KMS Litho, Hook Norton

Contents

Acknowledgments

To my mother, whose words of caution to 'Walk humble, my son' I have not, to my cost, always heeded, my loving remembrance and gratitude.

To my grandson, Gary Moss, whose artwork on the cover is a brilliant depiction of myself as a boy, my mother, my then home and birthplace, and the churchyard, family graves and the entrance gates which gave our cottage its name of 2, Church Gates; with, too, the cause of my mother's words, the irate man at the gate with whom I had had an acrimonoius slanging match: Well done and thank you, Gary, I hope you go far in your career, from Grandad.

To Carole Angier of High Street, Ascott-under-Wychwood, whose friendly care and guidance during the process of publication enabled this book to be produced, my sincere thanks.

To Sue Jourdan and Wendy Pearse of the Wychwoods Local History Society, my thanks for their support of my work; to John Rawlins of the Wychwoods Local History Society, to Eric Pratley of Ascott-under-Wychwood and to Ralph Mann, thanks for their help with photographs.

To the Greening Lamborn Trust, and I hope in future also to the Marc Fitch Fund, both of Oxford, my thanks for their financial support of the publication costs.

To my publisher, Jon Carpenter of The Wychwood Press, Charlbury, my thanks for his faith and interest in this book.

Last but not least, thanks to my readers, who I hope will enjoy it.

Eric R. Moss

Dedicated to my descendants

'Walk Humble, My Son'

I WAS BORN in the village of Ascott-under-Wychwood in Oxfordshire on April 30th, 1918, in the sign of Taurus theBull, in a small stone cottage to the right of the churchyard entrance gates. It was known as No. 2 Church Gates and was then the property of Cornbury Park Estates.

I arrived in this world at the same time as hundreds of thousands of people were leaving it due to the agonies of the Great War — and the Spanish influenza, which was sweeping all over Europe.

The war was not going well for England just then; my father, Ernest Walter Moss, and two of his brothers were away at the war front and my mother was left at home with six other children when I came along. Times were very hard.

My eldest brother Ernest had left school at the age of twelve in order to help out on the farms and to bring pence for the family purse, while my elder sister Ruth went into domestic service.

With the war there was a great shortage of labour everywhere, especially on the farms which were labour intensive. Many men, boys and women were required to do the amount of work which today is done by the farmer and perhaps his son, or one other, with the help of much expensive machinery.

The coming of steam to the fields

In those days shire horses did most of the work because tractors and steam engines were few in number. Steam traction engines powered large lorries and also ploughs, and locally were supplied by the Griffin Bros. of Bruern Grange Farm, and by Baileys of Lechlade. These men were farmers and agricultural contractors who supplied steam traction engines to haul and drive threshing machines and to power steam ploughs. With a large steel roller in place of the front wheels, these monsters became steam rollers for road repairs.

As ploughs, two engines would be employed, one at either end of the field, with a mobile plough steered by a man sitting on it being pulled to and fro between these engines on large steel ropes.

When water or coal was required, the engine drivers would sound their steam whistle and the farmer would hurry the fuel to them. Much of the coal came from trucks standing in the siding at Ascott railway yard. The coal would be put into horse waggons which had previously been weighed on the weighbridge just inside the station yard entrance. When filled, the waggon and its coal would be weighed again and a ticket issued from the little brick hut alongside the weighbridge where the scales could be read. Both weigh-bridge and its hut disappeared in the late fifties under the Beeching Plan.

A plough with a single shear, pulled by two large shire horses, did a good day's work to plough one acre to a depth of about seven inches. The steam plough could plough more and deeper and often on the Cotswold hills would do more harm than good when it ploughed too deep and pulled up large 'rugg' stones from the subsoil. Top soil would be lost in the cavity made and extra labour had to be employed to pick up the stones. This type of plough died out when petrol driven tractors became plentiful, but it has to be admitted that there was no better tool for breaking up gorse or furze land than the steam plough.

Spanish flu and the death bell

The Spanish flu was so called because it started in Spain before sweeping through the whole of Europe, killing an estimated 40 million people world-wide. My mother said that the 'death bell' was ringing from the Church almost daily while the plague raged. As an infant I was lucky to escape the grim reaper, but one such child, Florence Maycock, did not; she died aged 10, and in 1990 her grave is still kept immaculately tidy by unknown hands.

The death bell was rung by the sexton, Mr. James Edginton — or 'Pecker' as he was nicknamed because of the short-handled pickaxe he was often seen carrying when he was grave digging. The bell was rung by that small plain rope just inside the belfry door on the left side. It was rung on the death of a villager at 'one for a man, two for a woman, three for a child'; that is, if a woman died two solemn 'dongs' would follow each other as the sound of the first faded, then there would be a pause of thirty seconds and another two 'dongs'. This would continue for about fifteen minutes, or longer if the bereaved were prepared to pay for it. On the day of the funeral the death bell would toll about every fifteen seconds for some ten minutes before the service.

This practice ceased on the death of the sexton after World War II, to cut costs and because people no longer wanted it. It is a pity in a way as it signi-fied just another break with the past and another rupture of the ties which bound villager to villager. Today this is a village of strangers: there are only about twenty-one village people that I knew fifty years ago. The last ten years have thinned us out. I am now the oldest Ascott member of the oldest Ascott family: we go back to the Civil War.

I am a direct descendant of a John Moss senior, though his son John Moss junior, who married Ann Brookes of Ascott in 1683, Ann dying in 1732. Their grandson William Moss, baptised 1736/7, and his second wife Sarah Lea, whom he married in 1766, were the parents of William Moss, baptised 1772, and Susannah Scaresbrook of Witney, baptised 1775. Through one of their ten sons, Thomas, who was baptised in 1798 and later married Anne Wiggins of Leafield in Ascott in 1823, came my grandfather Walter Moss, baptised 1839, brother-in-law to Jane Honeybone, a gloveress of Ascott who was born in 1842 and married my grandad's brother Robert in 1862. She was one of the 'Ascott Martyrs' – of whom more later.

In the 1881 census there were 71 Mosses in the village of about 250 people. When I was six years old there were still eleven Moss families in Ascott; now there is only one, my parents' descendants.

The railway and its work

Ascott Station was opened in 1853, after the building of the embankment which now forms the level crossing. The road from Chipping Norton ran in that boggy patch over the boundary wall to the cricket field and edge of the railway allotments, coming out by the Churchill Arms. A pond was dug out there about 1985 for ducks and wild birds. The river crossing prior to the coming of the railway was a ford where there is now a bridge.

Between the wars there was a train of some sort every half an hour on this busy Worcester line, most being goods trains filled with coal and having the name of the Coal Pit painted in 12 inch high letters on the waggon sides. We had a siding at Ascott station yard, and often in the night we could hear the whistles, clanks and clangs of trucks being shunted into that siding for unloading.

Always some of these trucks contained coal for the power station of the Langley G.P.O. Wireless Station with its 308 foot tall steel tubular poles or masts. Men climbed up inside to reach an exit near the top where they got into a bosun's chair to be pulled up the last few feet to repair the red aircraft warning lights or the aerials on top of the poles. It is said that the first message received by this wireless station was the news of the Battle of Jutland.

As a child at school I often watched a man called Wiggins from Leafield and his team of six black horses and waggon trotting past the school towards the station, and getting into a gallop as they passed the Churchill Arms public house in order to get up the steep approach slope to the station yard and its coal sidings. After he had turned his waggon round in the yard he would pull alongside a railway truck and load coal into his vehicle. After his waggon had

Eric's parents, Walter Ernest Moss and Rosa Scarfe, on their wedding day in 1904.

been weighed he would slowly walk his team back past the pub and then start them into a trot for the long haul past our schoolyard up the hill called London Lane to the crossroads at the top where, having turned right on to a level road, they would walk slowly to get their breath again before turning left for the long uphill haul to the wireless station, some two and a half miles from Ascott. This journey the team did twice a day, five days a week. The water heated by this coal passed through the turbines into a brick-lined pond to be re-used. The pond made an ideal swimming pool for the staff.

This coal hauling ceased when the 308 foot high poles were felled in 1963 or thereabouts, replaced by smaller 120 foot lattice masts with new buildings and mains electricity. These lattice masts have now gone too, and the premises became a school for the GPO wireless department and more recently a site for the TWR Group.

After the first world war my father worked on the Great Western Railway and was based at Ascott, which then had a large number of men working as relaying gangs. These gangs also cut the grass on the embankments and cuttings, cleaned out the drain ditches which followed both sides of the double tracked embankments and cuttings, repaired fences and did all kinds of manual work. They were often carried by rail to do work elsewhere such as clearing the lines when wet weather caused the sides of cuttings to slide down and block the lines. Other men worked in the signal box, continuously manned for 24 hours a day and needing six full-time signalmen.

At Ascott-under-Wychwood both the up (to Oxford) and down (to Worcester) lines had a platform and a substantial wooden waiting room. The waiting room on the down line had a fire and doors to keep it warm. This room adjoined the wooden house lived in by the station master, and also the ticket office. There was also a brick toilet block which together with the rest of the public rooms, was cleaned by one of the two full-time ticket collectors-cum-porters.

Trains stopped at least every two hours to drop passengers for Leafield, Finstock, Lyneham, Chilson and other villages not served by Shipton or Charlbury. This state of affairs, with sometimes over 100 people waiting to catch the up train, ceased when Finstock and Combe had halts built for their use in the early thirties. These are still used today by a smaller number of people and there is only one rail track now and no goods trains. This loss of trade for Ascott Station meant a reduction in station staff. Now tickets are obtained on the trains, and the signal box shuts at 10 o'clock at night. There are few stopping trains and no goods traffic.

The normal weekday saw Dad off to work at seven after a cup of scalding hot tea. He reported to his ganger or foreman at the railway station, and with a 14 lb sledge hammer on his shoulder and a sandbag full of octagonal shaped hardwood blocks about nine inches long, he would walk the down line to Shipton-under-Wychwood Station.On his way he had checked that all the existing blocks were tight in their 'chairs', which is the name given to that large chunk of metal which holds the rail to the sleepers.If he found a loose block he would hit it back with his hammer unless it had worn or shrunk to the extent that it needed to be replaced; he would do this from the stock in his sand bag. The faulty blocks were supposed to be handed in to the railway store for checking but many found their way to our fire and jolly good burning material they were too.

In very hot weather many blocks would shrink and be vibrated out of their chairs by passing trains. This could be very dangerous and it was essential that all should be checked daily. Nowadays there is a continuous rail of different design and section from that of my youth; the sleepers are now of concrete, not wood, and the blocks as used by Dad have been replaced by large flat pieces of spring steel bent into an S shape and hammered home between chair and rail. In the old days these rails were reversible and when one 'bull-nosed' running surface was worn, the sixty-feet long rails would be unbolted at the 'fishplate' covering the joint, the blocks would be removed from either side of the rail and the rail turned over to be rebolted and blocked.

The average adult stride is about thirty inches, that being a soldier's stride or pace, but railway sleepers are laid at about twenty-seven inch centres, and this makes walking on the railway extremely tiring.

The active life of a sleeper was reckoned to be about twenty-four years, after which whole lengths of line would be relaid, usually on Sundays. I remember when, as a schoolboy at Ascott, one year great piles of very black, smelly sleepers were stacked to the side of the down line about 300 yards past the signal box towards Shipton. The railway banks had been shorn of grass which then lay around being turned into hay. A passing train blew sparks from its chimney which ignited the grass; this in turn set fire to the sleepers. There was a terrific fire which also burnt the sleepers under the rails before the fire was put out by dozens of people with buckets, helped by older boys from the school and by railway men. Trains were delayed for many hours and had to proceed at a snail's pace over the damaged rails.

While talking to Mr. Stan Webb in October 1990, he told me that a similar fire started there in 1906. Stan died in November 1992, age 93.

Having got to Shipton, Dad would have a few words with the Shipton ganger and then start back on the up line. Dad kept his eyes open for pheasants or

Two views of Ascott station. Note in the upper picture that the waiting room on the up line (on the left) was built on stilts. People used to sit along the back of it to watch the cricket in the field below.

partridges, rabbits or hares, which had either flown into the telegraph wires along the railway, or had been knocked over by the train. These birds or animals were welcomed by mother to feed her family; the older children, who had to pluck the birds or skin and gut the rabbits and hares, were not so keen.

When Dad got back to Ascott he went home about 8.15, had his breakfast by 8.45, and was off again for four miles along the up line to Charlbury where he turned round and walked back to Ascott by the down line. This was a total of twelve miles of inspecting four wood blocks every two feet three inches of the way, a mind-boggling thought, but a job which was being done by thousands of men each day to make the railroads safe.

Dad's wages were sometimes boosted by Sunday work when his gang would be miles away with other gangs relaying lengths of railway track or realigning existing track. When working close to home the sounds of dozens of shovels, pushing and tamping the ballast tight under the sleepers, would be heard for hundreds of yards and sounded like sharp sand being shaken inside a coconut shell. Sometimes his gang would be called out to move earth 'slipped' on to the line in cuttings, and I remember when Chipping Norton line and tunnel were blocked by such a 'slip', and Father had to lodge at Hook Norton for a fortnight until the job was finished.

When a gang was working on the tracks there was a 'safety man' a hundred yards away between the gang and oncoming trains, who was armed with red and green flags and a very strong whistle. If the work was more important than mere routine maintenance, the trains would be slowed by detonators placed on the line which made a bang many times louder than a shotgun.

Often in very foggy weather Dad or one of his mates would have to go 'fogging', an all-night duty which involved laying these detonators on the rails about a mile outside Ascott Station in the direction of Charlbury. (A detonator looked like a rounded tin of boot polish with four-inch lead straps either side to hold it on the rail top.) The exploding detonators warned the train drivers that they were approaching Ascott station and would have to slow down in readiness either to stop for passengers or shunt trucks or to reduce speed over sections of line being worked on. Sometimes it was necessary for Dad to stop the train and talk to the driver in which case he would go several hundred yards towards Charlbury and fix his detonators. He then laid another a hundred yards nearer his hut and then three more a few yards only apart. The first bang alerted the driver and the second bang slowed the train until the three bangs close together caused the brake-locked engine wheel to throw out showers of sparks as the train came to a halt. Dad also had an oil lantern with red and green shutters, so that he could use a red emergency light when necessary. Since signals were lit by oil they were hard to see in the fog and then only when the train was close to them.

If it got foggy in the afternoon and Dad was on this duty, Charlie 'Chips' Sherborne would call on Mum and explain that Dad would be fogging and would she send his tea to him. Very often I went, taking my younger brother, and Dad would allow us to stop for a while. We were thrilled by the bangs of the detonators and Dad's workman's hut which smelt of steam and creosoted wood from the old sleepers used for firing.

Sometimes when Dad stopped a train, the fireman would tip a few shovels of coal onto the ground for use in the hut, but some of this would find it way home. It was steam coal and not so good on the domestic fire as the 'cobbles' bought from Marriott's 'Feed and Coal' dump in our station yard.

There were two tracks to the railway of my youth and two large waiting rooms, one for each platform. There were a ticket office, a bricked toilet block and a station master's house all made of wood with blue slated roofs, and painted in brown and beige. All these buildings have gone now; there is only one track from the crossing up to Oxford and one glass bus-stop type waiting room for the few passengers who now use the two stopping trains of the day. Only the signal box remains of the old railway station; even the crossing gates, laboriously opened and shut by the large wheel in the signal box, have been replaced by continental type barriers which stand bolt upright when not in use. Television screens enable the Ascott signalman to open and shut the barrier gates at Bruern crossing four or five miles away, and soon both Ascott and Bruern will be opened and shut by TV from Oxford. Such is alleged progress; I wonder what the ghosts of the old railway men will do about it as they watch the scene where their aching bodies laboured so hard for so little, so long ago.

Up to about 1933, when 'halts' (or basic platforms for passengers to alight from or ascend the trains) were built at Finstock and Coombe, there would be up to one hundred passengers or more on Ascott's platforms as people from Leafield and surrounding villages used this public transport to Oxford and London. The motor car and poor passenger services have almost killed this railway which no longer carries goods trains.

At one time the little railway station at Ascott boasted a station master with a decorated hat and tunic, and also at least one permanent porter-cum-ticket collector. Six signalmen did shift work in their box which was then manned twenty-four hours per day. They also provided relief labour at other boxes. I can remember two station masters, Mr. Attwood and Mr. Lloyd. Sadly they and the old time signalmen, the coal trucks and black horses, the steam trains and the camaraderie of the railway have gone, leaving only ghosts and a few faded photographs as memories.

Cottage life

The cottage I lived in was more or less the same as dozens of others in the village. Most of them were tied cottages for the many men who worked the land. There were two bedrooms in ours, reached by a semi-circular flight of built-in treads and risers in what had once been an ingle nook in the chimney breast of a larger house before it had been divided into two cottages. My father said it had once been a farmhouse belonging to a small farmer whose land had been swallowed up by Cornbury Estate.

Mother and Dad slept in the smaller of the two rooms which was about twelve feet by twelve, and had one small window overlooking the churchyard. This window was fitted with very old blacksmith-made iron-framed leaded lights of diamond shaped green glass. These lights hung on the old fashioned 'hook and ride' hinges as were fitted to the wooden field gates of those days. Thirty-seven years later this was the larger room of a three-bedroomed house, as I practically rebuilt the interior of it for my widowed mother. It was given another window overlooking the back garden and railway. Mother's bed was a large double feather bed with iron bedheads having loose brass knobs which chattered when a steam train ran at speed on the railway 150 yards away.

When, as small children, we were unwell — which was often — we were taken into this bed to sleep between Dad and Mum. I still remember the many times I slept there, with a blocked nose and a headache listlessly listening to the everlasting chatter of a slow, long goods train as it rattled past our house. On those sleepless, feverish nights I heard the screech of the Screech Owls as they searched the churchyard, or the too-whoo of the Barn Owls in the church belfry. Sleep only came to me when Dad left the bed for work at six in the morning.

The ground floor of our cottage had two rooms, the 'front' and the 'back' room. Most of our family life centred around the front room with its cooking range fire and oven. The usual oval shaped cast iron cooking cauldron hung from a chain up the chimney, positioned over the fire. This cauldron had in earlier days held a continuous supply of thin soup to which any edible oddment of food was added. In my younger days the cauldron was used mainly to heat water for baths which took place in a tin bath placed before

Left to right: Percy Charles, Vera May, and Eric.

the fire. For the first fourteen years of my life no heat existed in the back room which became a secondary storeroom for wet clothes and dirty boots.

When I was about fourteen the Cornbury Park Estate Office decided to build a copper in this room, an event which had the advantage of providing some form of heat on the occasions when the copper was used for washing or heating bath water. In the latter case the bath was used in this room, but the young bodies were dried and prepared for bed in the front room.

The disadvantage of the copper was the steam which went everywhere and smelt while making everything wet. It also took up a lot of room and sometimes when the wind was in the wrong direction the room was full of smoke. By the time I was sixteen, this copper was removed and built again in the 'hovel' — which is what we called our stone-built store shed sited twenty feet from our back door and adjoining the building used by 'Slasher' Moss to cut his chaff and store his horse cart.

This hovel was used to store potatoes and the railway sleepers which were sawn up in it and then split into kindling wood for the daily fires. This sleeper sawing and splitting was one of the regular chores the boys of twelve and over; each had to do in his turn. Our many cycles and gardening tools were stored here; the hovel had no window and only a dirt floor. I was to alter this in later years.

Fuel for this copper was anything burnable, including slack coal which was almost dust, potato peelings, cardboard boxes, and the twigs and small pieces of rotten wood blown from the many trees lining the roads. This was brought home in the women's aprons when taking their children for an airing, or on the front of the prams.

As there were thousands of elm trees lining both the roadsides at about ten yard intervals, and very little motor traffic, there was usually no difficulty about collecting firewood. Often the

Elm trees lining the Chipping Norton road.

pram with a baby in it would be loaded with dead fallen branches, broken roughly to length and placed across the body of the pram to hang over the sides by about two feet.

Every high wind brought down elm trees which were shallow rooted and often they fell across the roads. In no time the fallen monster would be surrounded by old men, women and children with axes, saws, sacks, prams and wheelbarrows, all trying to get as much wood as possible before the authorities got there with their long two-handled saws to cut up the tree, and their chains and horses to pull the pieces aside to open the road.

We of course had Dad's ration of sleepers, which made ideal kindling wood but burnt too quickly if used as logs. All workers on the railway were entitled to an annual ration of one ton of old, time-expired sleepers, as the wooden railway ties were called. For this ration my father in the early days paid 7/6d or about a quarter of his weekly wage. The price crept up until by 1945 he was paying £1 for his ration, still about one quarter of his weekly wage. Dad's ton of worn sleepers meant about twenty average sleepers, or more if some of them had got rotten due in part to bad 'pickling' with creosote before use.

Power for a pound

Electricity came to Ascott-under-Wychwood about 1933, and was installed by the Wessex Electricity Company, a private concern who supplied four lights and a 15 amp plug for one pound. The actual house wiring was done by Charlie Bridgeman from Milton-under-Wychwood with lead covered wires. As wages then were about 32/- per week for my father, that £1 was quite a sum of money. Today this wage of 32/- would be expressed as £1.60 for 48 hours work. His gross wage today (in 1990) for 48 hours work would be £123.

The telephone with its hundreds of poles came to Ascott and its neighbouring villages about 1929. Hundreds of black, sticky, smelly, creosoted poles and thousands of cross bars about 5 feet long for fixing to the tops of the poles were dumped on the village green. These held the cups of white 'china' which tethered the phone wires to the poles without earthing them. These items, together with dozens of creosoted slabs of timber about 3 feet long and lengths of half round timber pointed at one end to lay on top of stay wires, made wonderful building material for young boys when they came out of school. Soon wooden forts sprang up everywhere made out of those 'cup' holding cross bars, and Indian yells were mixed with the bang! bang! bang! of the defenders as games of 'Settlers and Indians' took place. A different yell and a different game was played by most of the boys and some girls when they got home and their mothers saw the awful mess the children had got their

Eric's birthplace. The photograph was taken in 1911 or before.

bodies and clothes into from that black creosote.

The poles were erected along the side of the road at 66 feet intervals and bright copper wires were soon strung between them. This brightness soon turned to green, then a blackish colour, as weather acted on the copper. These wires became a favourite perch for swallows when they collected together at the end of summer for that long journey to Africa.

Early memories

When I was six months old I nearly died from sunstroke, my sister having failed to put up the hood of my pram as she wheeled me around the village in the strong sun. When I was born, babies were wrapped in 'swaddling' clothes and kept in their prams for months; indeed a child was treated as a baby until he or she was almost one year old.

My earliest recollection of my young life was of the day my mother had me cradled in her arms holding me with one hand while she cut and ate two cold sausages from an old fashioned white enamelled plate with a blue rim. Mother was singing 'Mademoiselle from Armentières' as she moved around the room, probably late in 1919. I remember mother offering me a piece of sausage and myself pushing it away screaming 'Gogah! Gogah!'

We had an old dog who roamed the garden. One day I had crawled out of the back door and was about to pick up a dried dog's dropping when my mother snatched me up and said, 'No! No! That's Gogah.' That sausage had reminded me of her warning.

Next door lived the Cooks, Charlie and Ada and their three children, two boys and a girl. My relations with them in later years was anything but cordial, but in my early years I got along with them very well.

As soon as I could walk I rapidly became more independent; actually it was a case of having to, as other additions were made to the family, four more in fact, making eleven in all.

Finding work

Once the eldest children left school they were put out to work. The girls went into domestic service in one of the local large houses, until they were old enough to go further afield and eventually to London. There they learnt airs and graces we in the country knew nothing about, and cared for less when they were tried out on us.

Rose, my eldest sister, had found a job with a very frugal, penny-pinching family, and became an apt pupil, perhaps because in self-defence she had no option. If my mother had an occasional few days with her sisters in Norfolk, we, the younger children, would feel the full weight of Rose's London education. Sitting still on chairs, wiping feet, cleaning shoes and of course washing the neck and behind the ears, were pretty soon followed by combing the hair and saying 'please' and 'thank you'. These were but a few of the travails we had to endure, the worst being at meal times when we noticed that the food portions had become smaller than those doled out by mother but, to cap it all, we had to leave a little food on the side of the plate on the pretext that we had had more than enough. This meant that no 'seconds' were offered, but if they had been we were told to refuse politely and say we were full up. We were all glad as children when mother came back and Rose went back to London, although we were always glad of the little gifts she somehow managed to bring us when she came home.

The boys went to the local farms until they could either find another job or went away with the farmers they were with, when those farmers changed farms.

Olave and Bill both went Banbury way; Olave went to Wroxton for two years until the farm was dug up for iron ore, when he went to the aluminium factory for the rest of his working life.

Poor Bill took over Olave's old farmhouse cottage and got a farm job. Bill had a double row of teeth until he was thirty when one row was removed. Because of his teeth he had a speech impediment, and perhaps was not as bright — or I would say as lucky — as the rest of us. In any case Bill and our father could not get on while the rest of us were so concerned with our own affairs that we did not support him as much as perhaps we should. Bill felt his position and eventually went away and severed all links with his family. Such attempts as were made to find him were fruitless.

Brother George went to Oxford to St. Edward's School as playing ground staff, where he was taught the games learnt by the pupils and he became very good at them. Later on George went to Littlemore Mental Hospital as a male nurse, and spent his happy life there travelling the world while escorting wealthy patients on their travels.

Singing in bed

All this meant that the most people I can remember in the cottage at one time were eight, including Mum and Dad. This was far too many when the weather was bad, and so the youngest of us were sent to bed as soon as we had had our early tea. Many wet or cold nights saw us in bed by five o'clock with only a flickering candle stub for company.

In bed we sang hymns or talked over the school day until the door at the bottom of the stairs would open and a voice would advise us to cut out the noise or else. In the winter this early going to bed was not too bad as I and my two younger brothers slept in one bed and kept fairly warm with a liberal layer of our coats on top of the blankets. Often we slept head to toe in an attempt to stop the spread of infection when mumps, chickenpox and measles were about, but to no avail — we all got our share of whatever came our way.

Each bed had a chamber pot under it and it was the job of the two eldest children to empty these into a bucket and dispose of the contents. This job was done daily. Although this was a hated job, it was not hated as much as the task of emptying the bucket standing under the seat in that building thirty yards down the garden path, as it often meant disturbing earlier burials of the same nature. Dad sometimes did it but the eldest boy was expected to dig the hole, empty and rinse the bucket, and put some Jeyes fluid in the bottom. This job was often done by me four times a week at the age of twelve.

There always seemed to be a child in the cot in Mum's room and it was one of the many irksome jobs given to the school-aged children to rock this cot and get its squalling occupant to sleep. This cot had been home made many years ago and comprised four legs about three feet high with the bed slats nailed on to rails mortised into the legs and fixed with a nail through the tenon. The top rails were nailed on top of the legs and the side slats were nailed top and bottom with a single nail each end. This allowed the cot to move out of shape when pushed and pulled, and this caused the necessary rocking motion. This, together with the squeaks of wood slats rubbing on wood rails, produced a sound which helped Morpheus to do his work. With luck the child would doze off while the 'rocker' would tiptoe towards the door in an attempt to escape. No such luck: at the threshold, the 'rocker' would be halted by a howl from the cot and would have to go back and rock the rickety, cumbersome cot again but this time with a little more and venomous vigour. This room would be lit by a guttering candle and had the faint smell of Cologne and talcum powder — the only signs of luxury in the house.

This bedroom and the front room downstairs were repapered about every three years with cheap 3d-a-roll, rose patterned wallpaper. In today's money that is just over 1p a roll. Mother did the papering, using her mixing bowl for the paste of flour and water. She smoothed the paper down with a handful of rag. The selvedge of the paper was cut off with scissors, which was a monotonous and mind-absorbing occupation not recommended for the ham-fisted.

The very large bedroom and the back room below were coloured with what was known as distemper, a coloured liquid which on drying left a powdery surface which came off on the hands. Available colours (since it was given free by Cornbury Park Estate) were a bright red, a very hard dark blue and green. Sometimes we were lucky and got a yellow. The ceilings were done with a ball of whiting, that is a ball about 5 inches in diameter composed of whiting, a chalk-like substance. This was crushed, put in a bucket with water to which Recketts Blue was added. The whole mixture was well stirred before being applied with a grass brush. This type of ceiling colour could be freshened up by brushing clean water over it but had to be stabilised or totally removed before the application of modern emulsions. Recketts Blue (in a small cloth bag the size of an egg) and Robin's Starch were famous laundry aids at wash day rituals, which took place on Monday for certain and on other days of course if the weather or family needs required.

Recketts Blue had other uses: it was considered good as an antidote for bee stings, and I remember one humorous occasion when it was used for that purpose. Our local 'heggler', Mr. Parkes, the egg purchaser who went from chicken keeper to chicken keeper to collect eggs for resale, was attending to the needs of nature when a bee landed on his credentials and stung him. Any bee sting is painful, in Mr. Parkes' situation it was very very painful, and he enlisted his wife's help with a bag of Recketts Blue. Mrs. Parkes sold second-hand paperbacks, and I was a voracious reader who had called to buy at the wrong moment and saw the proceedings. As Mr. Parkes opened his trouser flies, Mrs. Parkes took a swipe at the affected parts with the Blue bag instead of trying to fix the bag to the sting with a bandage. One would have thought these two were strangers instead of man and wife of many long years.

I can remember the time our house was roused in the night to the cry of 'Fire', and fire it was in mother's bedroom. The candle had toppled over due to a draught and had set light to the plywood top of a bamboo table bought for 6/4d in 1904. I still have that old table and its price tag; it has a new plywood top but the old one complete with fire singed hole is visible underneath. A wooden case clock standing on the table was destroyed in the fire which Dad smothered with a blanket.

Weekend jobs

All the children in our house were bathed on a Saturday night in front of the fire and some were done straight from school so that the workers could see and enjoy the fire when they came home an hour or more later.

The flagstone floor of our living room was usually bare except by the fire. Sometimes mother would buy some cheap lino from hawkers at the door or from the Co-op roundsman, but it never lasted long. The uneven, well worn flagstones did not allow the lino to lie tight to its surface; there were always places where a toe could catch underneath the lino and the resultant trip would tear it. Soon that piece would be taken up until mother could afford coco matting, as coir matting was called. Usually this was plain with the cut ends covered with a bit of cloth to prevent fraying. It lasted longer but collected all the dust and dirt imaginable.

One of Saturday morning's jobs for us children, if it was fine, was to remove this matting to the clothes line outside and give it a good beating while others swept the floor with our softest broom, so that mother could scrub those flagstones. When the floor was dry, old newspaper was put down if available, and then the matting, after mother had inspected it to see how well or not we had beaten it, was laid on top.

In front of the fire was a spark guard if wood was being burnt and outside this was the 'child guard', a blacksmith-made three-foot high metal fence with three-eighths of an inch iron bars fixed to the top and bottom rails every four inches or so. The ends of this metal fence were bent at right angles about fifteen inches in at both ends, the top rail of which had a small downwards pointing piece of three eighths inchbar about three inches long which was dropped into holes in spikes driven into the fireplace surround. This guard served a dual purpose, stopping children falling on the fire and providing somewhere safe to hang wet clothes when the workers came home.

In front of this guard was put a rug made by mother from a washed hessian sack cut down the sides and stitched all over with coloured pieces of cloth about four inches long and one and a quarter inches wide. These cloth pieces were cut from old clothes and were stitched through the hessian with a pointed awl which had a movable jaw. When a lever under the handle was pressed the jaw was opened and the end of a piece of cloth was inserted. When the handle was released, the jaw shut tight on the cloth which was then pushed through the hessian through the double hole made by the awl's point. Once the material was through the hessian it was pulled hard to make both ends past the double hole equal on each side. Patterns were made by using coloured bits of cloth and the rug, when first made, gave a small touch of luxury to the room which otherwise was very basically furnished. There was an expanding deal table, six wooden chairs of the cheapest type and a high backed wooden chair with arms for Dad. This had a cushion on its seat tied to the back to prevent slipping. Mother also had a smaller, high backed chair and cushion, but for some reason her chair had been treated with the black/brown varnish stain of the period.

There was a small net curtain to the bottom half of the front room window, which was so low that people going through the church gates could see everything in the room. At night, dark red plush curtains would be pulled along the iron curtain rod and the oil lamps or candles would be lit.

The mat described above could be found in most houses but they collected dust and were beaten with sticks every Saturday over that overworked washing line. Sooner or later this rug would be relegated to the back room for the purpose of wiping boots, prior to taking them off for cleaning over a bucket which collected the mud from the fields. There was of course a foot scraper outside, but when it was raining who could blame the poor devils of land workers for getting quickly inside to the comparative warmth of the back room? The land worker wore heavy hobnailed boots and his trouser bottoms were covered with First World War 'puttees' wound around the bottom leg for extra warmth, protection from knocks and to keep the trousers clean. Of course these puttees were covered in mud, which had to be scraped off so that the puttee could be hand washed and dried for next day's use. Some of these jobs were done by the older children to give mother a break.

On really bad days the copper in the back room would be lit to give some warmth and also hot water to wash not only the puttees, but trousers as well, as land work in those days in bad weather could be atrocious. Most men and boys wore ex-soldiers' overcoats and tunics as they were cheaper to buy than civilian clothes and probably a lot warmer and harder wearing. Sometimes bath night for the children was brought forward if the weather dictated that the copper would be lit.

Those nights of the late twenties when, as children, we had to go to bed early to make room at the fire for the workers, were enlivened by the smoking of cigarettes made from 'dog-ends'. These were found in my eldest brother's old trouser pockets; he had left these trousers hung on the bed irons after changing to go out. Thankfully no damage was done by this dangerous prank which would have resulted in the strap and a good smacking had we been found out.

A meal together

In the summer the family tried to take its evening meal together. This was the main meal of the day taken at a quarter past five and consisted of all types of vegetables grown on Dad's two acres of allotments, with meat from what he had managed to pick up on the railway or whatever my eldest brother Ernest shot, snared or netted in the evenings and weekends.

Sometimes in summer, if there were left-overs of vegetables, these would be eaten cold as a supper or kept for the next day when the schoolchildren had them warmed up for their midday meal. Dad and my working brothers had fresh food cooked for their evening meal. Breakfast was usually porridge with milk and sugar if the money ran to it, or salt or nothing if money was tight. I remember often going to school after eating a slice of thick bread smeared with shop lard used for cooking and with a small amount of sugar spread on it.

One thing cannot be disputed. Cottage gardens grew the best crops of the best vegetables grown in the village, due to the bucket and the deep black soil it created. Twenty years after the last bucket was destroyed, these back gardens still produced good crops. I'm sure that if the farmers used animal manure today, as they did between the wars, we would be a healthier nation. Nature's way is best.

Ferreting

Often in the winter evenings my brothers and I would knit rabbit nets with our home-made wooden needles and mesh gauge. We used twopenny balls of string because it was cheap, but it had drawbacks in being so thick and stiff. This warned the rabbits who could see it against the sky when coming out of their burrows, but the pursuing ferrets would force them to risk it and of course they lost out.

My brother kept about six ferrets and polecats. The difference between these was that the ferret was a light golden colour while the polecat, which was the same shape and size, had large brown all-over markings; both had pink eyes. Some were savage but usually they were so tame you would put them under your shirt or allow them to crawl along your shoulders and over your neck.

You caught your ferret or polecat by holding its attention with the fingers of your left hand held about six to nine inches from its eyes, while your right hand went the long way behind him and came up to his neck which you grabbed close to the head. Some ferrets or polecats roamed loose in the burrows to find and drive out the rabbits. One did not feed these animals for hours before using them in order to make them keen to work. However, this sometimes worked against you and the ferret would kill a rabbit by biting the spine through at the back of the neck and then sucking the blood, after which it would lie up with its victim and go to sleep. This meant the loss of a valuable animal so another ferret, or usually a bitch polecat used to the job, would have a collar with a small bell fitted and a bricklayer's line attached to the collar. This animal would then be put down the hole nearest to where the missing ferret was last heard, and the line would be played out while one of the humans kept his ear to the ground. When the line stopped, spades or grafts would be used to dig back along the line until the two ferrets were found, and the victim was removed.

To attract ferrets back up a hole a man would suck through his teeth with his tongue pushed against the teeth. The resulting hissing, sucking sound usually did the trick and the ferret would come out.

In those days there was little or no tinned dog or cat food. Anyway it would have been too expensive for us to buy to feed cats, dogs or ferrets. We fed the ferrets with small birds caught at night with clap nets, until the day came when a bird-loving school teacher showed us the errors of our ways. Though we still caught the birds we put rings on their legs, logged the time, place, bird, sex and then let them go.

Bill Campbell and the shrike

That teacher was Mr William ('Bill') Campbell, who later taught in Charlbury and Shipton and wrote 'Nature Notes' for the *Guardian*. He died in November 1994. He once lived at High Lodge in Leafield parish, before moving to Priory Lane, Ascott-under-Wychwood. When I was sixteen I delivered letters to his family at High Lodge, where he lived with his mother, sisters and one brother who worked in Cornbury Park gardens (as did his father). One other brother, Ian, worked in London, I believe, while his elder brother, Ben, was a wireless operator spending six months of the year at sea in a whaling ship. On retirement this brother lived in a modified wartime prefabricated house moved from a clearance site in London and placed in Cutts Close, Ascott. This house had a brick wall of a single brick's thickness built round it to disguise it, and I put a pitched raftered roof on it and tiled it.

William Campbell also taught me at teachers' classes at the Central Boys' School, Gloucester Green, in Oxford, of which more later.

It was while William lived at Priory Lane that we caught a Great Grey Shrike while out clap netting, a procedure described below. William was so excited that we went straight to his home where he looked up his books to confirm his catch, while the bird sat docilely on my wrist. It appeared to me to be some kind of hawk. A few days later a rather long record of the bird's capture appeared in the local press, where we read that it was very scarce and that the last known specimen was shot at Banbury in 1880.

Clap nets were a pair of canes about three quarters of an inch in diameter, and about ten feet long. They were bent at the top like large hockey sticks and joined together at the ends with leather hinges. A light strawberry type of net was fixed to the canes' top half, while the bottom ends of the canes were used as handles. These nets could then be folded in half. They were used at night; we liked dark nights so that the birds could not see the net against the moon. The man with the net and a man with a torch went on one side of the hedgerow while the 'lusher' or 'lushers' (men with long sticks) went the other side. The net was opened close to the hedge and the torch was shone into the hedge so that the catcher could see the birds. The lushers on the other side would beat the hedge to frighten the birds into the net. When the birds flew out and were caught by folding the nets on them, the catcher called 'stop' and the lusher stopped hitting the hedge until the birds had been dealt with. The process was then repeated.

We did not kill all birds. Thrushes, robins, goldfinches, warblers and tits were released. Any large bird like a pigeon or pheasant was kept for the pot. The ferrets had the rest until the killing was stopped, and then we had to feed the ferrets with badly shot rabbits, rabbits intestines, and any rat or mouse which was caught. We also fed them on bread and milk.

The business of rabbit catching was almost universal amongst the labouring classes who formed the bulk of Ascott-under-Wychwood's 250 inhabitants. Without rabbits the meat intake of the working villagers would have been almost non-existent, as butcher's meat was so expensive.

Rabbit catching was a farm labourer's perk given him by his boss to subsidise his wages, and to keep down the plague of rabbits which seemed to infest all farms but which were treated in the inter-war years as another crop. The sale of rabbits to the Co-op even paid a man's wages for one farmer I knew. Rabbit skins fetched anything from 2d to 4d, and even 6d at the time of the outbreak of World War II, when agricultural wages were 32/- per week.

Pigeon shooting

Another source of meat was pigeon shooting. Vast flocks of hundreds of pigeons would descend on a field of wheat and eat a pound of grain each per day, or they would attack the greenstuff like kale grown for the sheep. A dozen pigeons would eat enough kale to feed at least one sheep. Today the large flocks have gone; pesticides on the vegetation and the close cutting of the once tall hedgerows have cut down the numbers of 'squabs' reared each year. Squabs are young pigeons and in a normal year up to four pairs of squabs would be reared. Each bird would eat its own weight of food twice a day, doing as much damage as a rabbit.

My brother George would come home to Ascott on his days off from his work in Oxford, and either went fishing, usually catching a 6 lb pike, or went shooting rabbits or pigeons. When he went pigeon shooting he used a decoy, either an artificial one or a dead pigeon with its eyelids cut off and propped up on a small forked twig facing into the wind on a suitable field. We would take cover in the hedgerow by an alder bush if available, with a twig covered hurdle for cover, and wait for the pigeons. On a good day my brother would shoot up to, and sometimes over, a hundred birds in a day. This meant that I would have to cycle five miles into Charlbury to get more cartridges at 2/6d ($12^1/_2$p) for a box of 25. In 1990 a box of twenty-five 12-bore cartridges cost about £2.50.

Often the dead pigeons, tied with binder twine about the necks in bunches of a dozen or more, would have to be thrown away because they had become fly blown which would soon turn into maggots.

We seldom got more than 2d or 3d for a pigeon, which just covered the cost of cartridges. Pigeon flesh is inclined to be very dry. My poor mother would treat them like poultry, and pluck and clean them, roasting them with stuffing like chickens. Nowaways a sharp knife is drawn down both sides of the breast bone, the skin and feathers peeled back and the two lumps of flesh forming the breasts removed for cooking, while the rest, still feathered, is thrown away. Young rooks are treated in the same way and are supposed to be very good.

Village bread and butter

There was no sliced bread in my youth, neither was it wrapped. Bread came in many shapes and sizes and quite a number of villages had their own cottage bakery. We got a lot of our bread for about 4d a loaf from Kethrows the Baker at Shipton-under-Wychwood. Kethrows made the cottage loaf which was composed of two balls of dough, one small about the size of a large fist, fixed on the other one which was about three times as big. Then there was the tinned loaf, a rectangular loaf baked in a tin with a lovely golden brown crust which was much loved by our family. Finally, as far as we were concerned, there was the Colberg loaf, baked in a pudding basin shaped mould. This was over-filled with dough which had a deep cross cut into it. When baked this cross-cut top rose and made four lovely crusty 'tits' which, when torn off (not cut) and spread with a little of the farm butter which sometimes came our way, was a glorious, heavenly treat.

New bread of all kinds had great appeal to hungry growing youngsters and whole loaves disappeared during mealtimes. We were not so partial to stale bread, sometimes deliberately made so in order to make the bread go further.

The farm butter I mentioned was made by Mrs. Harry Chaundy at Manor Farm. Often when we were sent to collect a halfpenny worth of skimmed milk in a wide, open-topped, blue enamelled metal milk can, we saw Mrs. Chaundy at work patting and shaping that butter. She used two wooden 'bats' as I called them, which had rectangular blades about six inches by four, or maybe slightly larger. These bats had ridges on one slde which made rectangular patterns in the surface of the butter when it received its final pat. This butter sold at 6d a lb. and was delicious. The skim milk we were after was a by-product of the butter making.

To get to the farmhouse we had to go over the level crossing at the signal box and through the little wicket gate which led to the path alongside the line, past some more of Dad's allotments, to another wicket gate in the railway boundary fence. From this gate there was a straight path to the farm. There was also a large flock of geese who hissed at us as we passed, with the ganders running at our small figures, with wings flapping, neck outstretched, and bills opened, creating fear and terror in our young hearts. A nip or pinch from a gander's bill or beak was no laughing matter and we were always glad to get out of the field which we never entered alone. We were then about six years old and not much bigger than those ganders. Outside the gate and away from the geese we would swing that milk can over our heads; its thin metal handle had a wooden grip which revolved around the metal, allowing us to whirl it above our heads without spilling the precious milk.

Of course one day the inevitable happened. The can in mid-air lost its handle. The milk was spilt, the can broken... and we got a hiding as there was no milk for Dad's tea that night.

Kitchens before electricity

There was no electricity in those early days, and the only oil was smelly, dirty paraffin. There was coal gas made at the gasworks at Shipton-under-Wychwood, which was used for the hissing, noisy, gas lights of the rich houses, the church and chapel, and also for the hideous, heavy cast iron kitchen cookers of blue enamel which the better-off people had. There were no refrigerators to keep food fresh and safe. Most houses had a small cupboard (or small room in the larger houses) on the north side of the house, and shelves to store the food. Most often a large red/brown earthenware bread bin or dough-mixing pan or 'crock', with a cloth over it, held the meat and the butter, pig lard or margarine as the case might be. The cloth helped to keep out the flies which abounded the cottages, and a fine fly mesh over the larder window protected that route. We had to put up with the cloth covered crocks.

Margarine came in round rolls wrapped in paper and was as hard as cheese. It was impossible to spread the stuff unless it was warmed in the oven or a hot knife used. It came in various colours from yellow to orange and was pretty tasteless. I much preferred pig lard or dripping. Shop lard was a pure white grease in paper packets, was utterly tasteless and was used mainly for cooking.

Margarine began to improve in 1938 but was never as popular as the easily spread, better tasting modern stuff. Cornflakes were a novelty for us in our early years but had become more widely used in their basic form as we left our teens.

The importance of the pig

Pig lard was made from the 'leaf' or coating of fat which covered the stomachs of larger pigs. It was rendered down, that is cut up and heated until the fat melted, and was run into a vessel with a few herbs to add flavour, and left to set. This lard was very tasty and easily spread, even in winter time, and was like a refined dripping which was the drips from the melted fat of a cooked joint of meat.

It is rare to get pig's lard today because pigs are bred for lean meat and killed when in the bacon or pork size which is up to 8 score lbs weight. Pigs are weighed in 'scores' of 20 lbs per score, and in my younger days and up to the war pigs were rarely killed under 20 score if they were cottage reared. When as large as this, the heavy amount of fat on the back was sometimes rendered down to make lard.

Fat bacon was the rule and some families seemed to have got by on boiled bacon and cabbage for six days a week. Sunday might give a variation to this diet. I know of a family of Wiggins at Leafield who lived this way on very fat salt bacon and cabbage for the main meal of the day, every day.

The pig was the most important domestic animal of my youth; all households kept one or two, either to sell for cash or most often to kill for use in the cottage. Thrifty people would join Pig Clubs to buy feed in bulk and thus cheaper, and to get insurance cover against illness and disease in their animals. Usually the pigsty and its manure heap was situated not far from the cottage back door, the sty being of either stone, wood, brick or corrugated iron. The pens or outlets where the pigs were fed were often of huge slabs of stone up to three feet wide and four feet six long, let endways into the ground and fastened together at the top with iron staples.

Straw for the pig's bed was easily obtained as no straw was burnt in those days, and all stubbles were ploughed in. The straw, however, was seldom as 'clean' as it is today as corn crops usually had as many thistles, poppies, squitch grass, cornflowers, plantains, hogweed and docks as they had corn. It took the second world war to introduce, at Government expense, herbicides and pesticides into agriculture and thus improve the yield of the crops.

Straw was built into ricks, like hay and corn,and was usually thatched to keep it dry. Oat straw was also used for cattle feed as it was softer than the wheat straw used for thatching, while barley straw was used for bedding the animals. Nowadays in Oxfordshire, barley straw is used for cattle feed and wheat straw is used for bedding. There are now no ricks built and very few oats grown; oats were in great demand for horse feed before the second world war.

Food for the poor man's pig was anything edible thrown into a large open-ended beer barrel standing outside the back door and having a loose lid on which a galvanised scoop was usually to be found. This barrel, called the pig tub, stank of frowsty sour food kept liquid by the addition of water. At potato harvest all the small potatoes of ping-pong ball size and less, those potatoes gone green from exposure to the sun, and any that were damaged or slug spoilt, were cooked in the 'copper' described below, and tipped into this pig tub. Pea and bean pods were thrown into the pig trough as they were. Grass cut from roadsides was fed daily to the animals.

The copper was a cast-iron bowl about twenty to twenty-four inches in diameter built into the top of a brick cube about four feet square and about three feet high. This had a fire hole at the front containing bars on which the fire burnt directly under the copper, and a flue hole which led to an outside chimney. It was closed at the front with a cast iron door and a wooden lid covered the copper itself to keep in the steam and thus accelerate the boiling process. It was used for washing laundry, heating water for baths and scrubbing floors, boiling hams if we ever got lucky, and of course the pig food. Christmas puddings were also boiled in it.

As the potatoes boiled in the copper, there arose a not unpleasant earthy smell and small fingers would reach out and snatch a frothy covered potato floating on the top. Either the skin of the potato was rubbed off by the fingers, or it was eaten as it was by the ever hungry youngsters watching the potatoes boil. Often Dad would have to call a halt to this scrounging as we were eating valuable pig and fowl food. These potatoes could be mashed with 'toppings' and egg spice to make chicken feed. The boiled potatoes were tipped into the pig tub to swell the food within, which was fed to the pigs at the rate of three bowls of swill to one bowl of barley meal well mixed.

All vegetable waste from the house, bad apples and forgotten crusts went into the pig tub while grass was cut from the road verges, and any hogweed was collected with sow thistles and bindweed from between the rows of growing potatoes and was fed to the pigs. I remember once passing the sty and hearing the pigs snoring very loudly. It was daytime so I looked over at them to see why they were so soundly asleep. They were well out to the world, in fact they were drunk from eating the remains of mother's latest parsnip wine making. She had thrown the parsnip pulp into their troughs for feed.

A lot of wine making was done by the cottagers, as by most people, because the basic materials were always cheaply to hand in season. Wine can be made from almost any vegetable or fruit material with some sugar and yeast added. As Dad grew a lot of parsnips for the table, the excess naturally went into wine, especially as Dad had no other alcoholic drink in that period between the wars. He had come home drunk once when I was a very small child and I can still hear my mother saying, 'Ern, if you come home drunk again I will leave you.' So Dad kept away from the pubs until his sons came home on leave during the second world war and persuaded him to go along and have a drink with them.

Dad had suffered severely from constipation for many years, and I have known him take two teaspoons of Epsom Salts and put them straight into his mouth to crush and swallow. This made him bad tempered. Going to the pub with his sons became a nightly one pint habit which cured his constipation and, to mother's delight, made him much easier to live with. I can see them now washing up the dinner things together like Darby and Joan, when I came home on an infrequent leave from the R.A.F.

Killing the pig

When a pig was killed there was an air of excitement at the prospect of good eating for a while. Straw would be placed near the sty and a place swept for the butcher's stool. A cord with a noose was taken into the sty and the noose dangled in front of the pig's nose. As the pig opened its mouth the cord would be pulled in and over the top jaw. This started the pig squealing and fighting, but it was pushed and pulled to the stool where it was lifted on and the cord swiftly wrapped around its jaws. Another cord and noose would be slipped over the uppermost front leg and pulled back away from the butcher's knife and hand. With a bucket under its throat to catch the blood, the butcher cut the pig's throat. Soon its shudders and squeals stopped, its body went limp, and it was allowed to fall off the stool. The cords were untied and the pig rolled onto the prepared straw. It was covered with more straw and then set alight to be scraped with a large knife and brushed down with a stiff brush to remove all bristles. It was then turned over and the process repeated. The blood was sometimes used for black pudding but most often it was thrown away. In Italy it is poured into boiling water with herbs and allowed to congeal into lumps. It is then taken out and fried, making a very tasty meal.

The pig was then cut down the middle from throat to anus and the entrails removed and put in a tub for cleaning. The heart, lungs and liver were hung on the garden line to cool and stiffen and so was the 'leaf' from around the stomach. This was hung on the line wrapped around a wire coathanger.

Very little of the pig was thrown away other than the 'bile bag'. The legs would be cut at the joints and broken, the front rib cage cut and a wooden stretcher put inside the pig to open it up to the air. A sharp hook was stuck into its jaw and it was hung up on a beam somewhere under cover to cool and set. Next day the butcher would return and cut up the carcase into joints for salting in large shallow elmwood trays. These joints were liberally hand coated with salt, which was well rubbed in daily. Hams were salted likewise, being brushed with salt by hand daily for up to two months, the hams and sides being turned each day until they were lying in a mixture of salt and body liquids.

The sides were cut up and the pieces put on the bacon racks that hung from the central ceiling beam in most cottages. These racks were pieces of wood hanging a foot or more either side of the beam and spaced roughly a foot apart. Sometimes they were built into inside walls. Since most cottages suffered from smoke, and wood was the most common fuel, the bacon on the racks acquired quite a 'smoked' flavour if left there long enough.

There are still plenty of bacon racks to be seen. Most developers seem keen to keep these links with the past when they 'modernise' these peasants' cottages for use by wealthy townie incomers.

The entrails or chitterlings (smaller intestines) would be cleaned by squeezing out all the excreta and forcing water to flow through them from a pipe, or from a tap if there was one. Otherwise they would be turned inside out and then washed, this process being repeated for three more days until they were considered clean.

The chitterlings would then be plaited as one would a rope or girl's hair, and then all were boiled and allowed to cool and set. When cold they would be cut up and fried, or stuffed and baked according to preference. There were always takers for the chitterlings if the owner did not want them, and no-one was offended if they were offered them in uncleaned condition.

When the leaf and sometimes the back fat on the heavy pigs were rendered into lard, the liquid fat went through a strainer which caught minute pieces of flesh, etc. When well cooked, these were, and still are today, known as 'scratchings' and can be bought in most pubs. When the pig was cut up next day the pig's tail was usually given to one of the small boys who always hung around pig killings. This tail when scraped and cooked gave several mouthfuls of meat from the thick end where it had joined the pig. The pig's bladder was much coveted and sought after by the boys who saw to it that every boy got one in rotation. The bladder would be emptied of its contents, blown up and the neck tied. It was then hung up to dry, after which it could be used as a football, or as a 'fool's' toy by the Morris Dancers who were prominent in the village at that time, and who still abound in the Cotswolds.

Long bristles from the tail were sometimes saved for use by the village cobbler and the harness maker who put a bristle in the end of his waxed twine to guide the twine through the awl holes made to stitch leather.

The village butcher in my youth was John Walker who lived in the house occupied in recent years by Mr. Leslie Barnes (who died in 1991) across the yard from Longhouse Farm. Mr. Walker was a very stout man and partial to his ale. He did most of the pig and sheep killing in this and other villages.

His wife made brawn from boiled pig's heads and other oddments of meat best not too closely enquired into. She sold this and sausages to the villagers. There was usually a lot of stubbly burnt bristles in the flesh of this brawn which, when boiled, was allowed to set in a bed of gelatine. It could be sliced cold for sandwiches, but I did not care for it. It had to be made palatable by the use of pickles or chutneys as it had a pretty bland taste by itself.

Pig's trotters, which produce much gelatine when cooked, with the toenails removed at the time the pig was dressed, were a delicacy much sought after then, but are not so popular today.

Dad bought his young pigs for 7/6d each from Smallstones Farm near Chilson, and I remember having a ride in a donkey cart to collect them, not much of an outing but quite an adventure for a three-year-old boy who listened with interest to the grown men's talk.

Off to school

I started school at the age of five at the Church of England Elementary School at Ascott. The headmaster was Mr. Kinvig who taught the seniors in the larger of the two classrooms. His wife taught the juniors in the smaller classroom. There were other pupil teachers who stayed for a short while and then moved on. There was also a Miss Pratley from Lyneham who stayed many years.

On my first morning I wore my coat with the little fur collar and cuffs; it was of course a secondhand coat once worn by a child of the rich, but I was too young to realise the social stigma which this at that time implied.

I remember that I had cried and, as I was a little 'fatty', I could not understand how I would live through the morning with nothing to eat. Mother in desperation cut two thick slices of bread and spread them with margarine, wrapped them in newspaper, and put them in my pocket.

On arrival at school I was torn from my mother's grasp and the door was shut in her face. This started me howling again so I was pushed towards the tortoise stove to await attention after the class had been settled down. After prayers led by Mr. Kinvig, Mrs. Kinvig came to me and demanded, 'Well, boy, what is your name, and what have you in your pocket?' Without waiting for an answer she grabbed my shoulder with her left hand and pulled out my lunch with her right. She then used both hands to open the packet and inspect the contents which she promptly disposed of by putting them in the stove. From that moment I hated that ageing woman with her dark clothes and hat with its faded ribbons sitting on her grey hair. She had destroyed something my mother had made and I would not forgive her.

My time in that small room with Mrs. Kinvig was a long session of using plasticene which, through use, had now the single colour of grey. No instruction was given or inspection of any modelling carried out by the teacher. Then we were given trays of sand and a handful of seashells with which we were supposed to make letters of the alphabet, and then our initials with the shells. We levelled the sand with our hands, flicking a little at the child in front when teacher was not looking.

Half a century of changing Ascott children: the lower photograph was taken in 1939.

Then there was needlework for boys as well as glrls. We were given a piece of cloth about six inches by four, a large needle and red cotton thresd. We were told to sew a hem around this piece of cloth and our initials in the centre. We had little instruction or inspection of the work, and we always had to unpick it at the end of the lesson ready for the next day. I remember we were given tiny metal thimbles to use.

Plenty of village children went to school without breakfast and some there were who walked in all weathers the mile and a bit to Cooper's Mill or the mile and three quarters to the cottages at King's Standing, arriving at school wet through and hungry. With elm trees every ten to fifteen yards either side of Brasswell Lane, this was hardly a safe place to walk in very windy weather as elm trees blew over like ninepins. Quite a number of cars got crushed and people were killed on the roads in windy weather. This lane led to King's Standing where the Loders, Lomasses and Floyds lived, and these children brought their lunches with them but usually ate them long before midday. This meant a long day of waiting for food for young bodies who did not get home before a quarter past five.

Schoolchildren then often wore their elder brothers' and sisters' cast-off clothing and shoes. No boy turned up for school without holes in the elbows of his jumper or the backside of his trousers. The toes of his boots would be scuffed through with the wear from wall and tree climbing. I remember the shame I felt in having to wear my sister's white knee-length stockings because mine were worn out; and then her shoes which were mother's hand-me-downs.

Food brought to school by 'outsiders' as we called them (because they did not actually live in the village) was the usual thick slices of bread and dripping or pig's lard, with a chunk of 'mousetrap' cheese or a bit of boiled pig's meat. Drink was from the tap or from a bottle of cold sweet unmilked tea, the same mixture that in larger quantities sustained their fathers and working brothers while at work.

Just inside the double wooden entrance gates of our schoolyard stood an ancient oak tree almost on its last legs. It had no large limbs in its top, just the pathetic remains of them with tiny spindly bits of branches like brushwood on which appeared in due season a few tired looking leaves. I was about eleven years old when this giant was felled by Mr. J. Young, our builder-cum-undertaker. It was sad to see it go as it had been like a friend. We played games around it and, while sitting in our classroom, we saw all kinds of birds alight on it, resulting in arguments as to what they were.

Old men told me as I got older that there had been another oak tree in that schoolyard as well as a number of pine trees (or fir trees as they were called), along that wall between the school and the farmhouse next door. This would have been about 1870 or earlier.

Occasionally Mrs. Kinvig would administer punishment to her pupils, using a kind of home-made birch. This was made from splitting the end of a fifteen inch long piece of cane after tying red cotton many times at the base of the splits which were about nine inches long. The ends of the split slivers of cane were loosely tied together to allow them to spread without breaking off. When administered to the trembling palm offered for punishment, this implement left lots of angry red weals on the skin. While Mr. Kinvig was well respected, his wife was considered to be 'an old bitch'. She often left her watch at home and many times I was sent to the schoolhouse for it. The door would be opened by Miss Nellie Moss (daughter of 'Slasher Moss' mentioned elsewhere) in a white starched maid's apron. She was still wearing this type of 'badge of servitude' after the second world war when she and her sister were working for the Treweeks for a paltry 6d a day. Poor devils, they represented with their employers the last remaining link with the 'Good Old Days', and still voted Tory in spite of their atrocious under-payment. For them the world had stood still; they still 'walked humble' as my mother had once pleaded with me to do, and I haven't forgotten. To the end they also believed 'that them above us allus knows best'.

The alphabet was taught with the aid of a wooden-framed slate and a slate pencil; of course the multiplication tables were learnt by rote. We were not too sure of the 11 and 12 times tables when the time came to go to the 'Big Room' and a higher class. There were few pictures around the walls and little of the pupils' work was exhibited for parents to see when they came to the school.

In the Big Room we had singing lessons once a week. I hated being told to sing solo but enjoyed the sound of the whole class bashing out the old favourites. This classroom had a painting of Grace Darling saving shipwrecked sailors, a large map of the world with the British Empire marked in pink, and a glass cage with a stuffed curlew inside. A case of birds' eggs under glass and a painting of prehistoric animals like the sabre-toothed tiger and the mammoth adorned the opposite walls.

Our desks were ten foot slabs of pitch pine with a long groove on the far side for pencils. About every two feet this groove was interrupted by a hole about one and a half inches in diameter for the inkwells which were filled every Monday morning by the ink monitor. The ink was made by powder and water being mixed in a jug and then poured into the little white ceramic pots stuck in their holes. This desk slab was fixed to cast iron latticed legs, whose fixing to the wooden top was often loose, causing the top to move if a pupil fidgeted without thinking, or more often deliberately to annoy his fellows and spoil their writing. The seats were made in a similar way. A slab of wood fixed to iron legs which rocked when a boy or girl wriggled his or her bottom.

The girls wore white aprons with frills to their shoulders, white stockings and a variety of shoes of hand-me-down history. Hair was long and down the shoulders or plaited, while clothing was also of the hand-me-down variety when elder sisters and brothers sometimes got something new from the Co-op. These items then did the rounds of going to younger brothers in due course. Boys were usually clad in jerseys often with holes in the elbows. Sometimes a straight tie with coloured bands on it would be seen, but not often. Short trousers, usually cut-down elder brothers' trousers, were the order of the day, and long knee-length stockings worn about the ankles to hide the holes in them or because they had become stretched and loose with much use. I and many other boys sometimes had to wear a pair of our sisters' white stockings and endure the jibes of our fellows. Sometimes we even wore our sisters' shoes if our own were unusable due to wall and tree climbing. Our boots, when we had them, were of the hobnailed type with heel tips like those worn by soldiers. The schoolyard was bare of grass and covered with small stones about the size of walnuts which in wet weather were trodden into the earth beneath them, and then kicked loose as the ground dried.

The main hall or Big Room with its two teachers and classes had a high boarded ceiling sloping with the roof. Often the elder boys would bring in mud fixed to the instep of their boots and when the teachers went into the small room (for a cup of tea made by Mrs. Kinvig) the mud would be pulled out and thrown hard at the ceiling above the teachers' desks. It stuck there like the first attempts of a flock of swallows to build nests, until the day came when the mud dried and fell down on Mr. Kinvig. One startled glance at the ceiling gave away the whole game. The class became silent as Mr. Kinvig opened his desk and produced his cane. 'Lomas! Shayler! Hutton! Edginton! Out here in front, quickly now! Hold our your hands! Higher!' and thwack went the cane onto each palm as he walked up to the next boy. He had not asked whether they were guilty, they usually were and were the most frequent recipients of the cane. None of the boys cried, much as their hands hurt; they were not going to give the Gaffer — or 'Kelly' as Mr. Kinvig was known to his pupils — best, and already seeds of revenge were coming to their minds. Mr. Kinvig was born in the Isle of Man — hence the nickname.

Whenever the otter hunt met in the village, and middle-aged followers in plus-four trousers, long stockings and leather gaiters with strong boots, gathered on the green, there would be truants among the older boys. As the hunt, men and dogs, moved down to the river bridge it was an almost certain bet that the boys mentioned above would be tagging along, their thumbs stuck in the V at the end of their sticks, and just as certain that they would be the ones to get the stick next morning.

Fox hunting was another excuse for the afore-mentioned boys to be absent from school, as the hunt met on our village green for many years.

The singing lessons produced songs which had been sung down the ages, such as 'Now is the Month of Maying' or 'The Lover and His Lass', to be followed by 'The Rowan Tree', 'John Peel', 'The Ash Grove' and 'The Cuckoo is a Pretty Bird'. 'Widdicombe Fair' was allowed when Mr. Kinvig was in a good mood, and the whole Big Room joined in as it was impossible to get on with such work as 'Reading, Riting and Rithmetic'.

There seemed no end to the variety of songs sung, yet sadly they are seldom heard today. At Christmas we sang the old carols and we decorated the room with paper chains made from strips of wallpaper stuck together with a paste of flour and water. How the youngest enjoyed seeing their elders climbing up on chairs to hang these chains and bits of holly and ivy. Sometimes on the day that school broke up for the holiday, a few parents would come and join in the carol singing, with the Vicar and perhaps a school manager or two.

Our church bell ringers were much in evidence at Christmas time and as children we loved to hear them on Christmas Eve and New Year's Eve. There was a period of about three years when our bell ringers rang their bells to the tunes of some carols. I reckon the village as a whole loved to hear these bells ringing out carols, but as usual the few Tory 'diehards' who ran the village from behind the scenes had their way and this was stopped.

There were about a hundred children in the school in the years 1920 to 1926, when the numbers, already dropping, were practically halved because the Education Authority decided that Ascott's twelve-year-old pupils should go to Shipton-under-Wychwood C. of E. School. Our parents did not think much of the idea and stopped us going: we were on strike. The strike lasted six weeks when our parents were taken to court and fined £1. The strike collapsed, which is another story and I am once again getting ahead of myself.

Fleas and lice

In the school there were problems for staff, pupils and their parents which, thank heaven, are seldom borne by modern generations though occasionally mention of some shades of the old days is made in the press. I refer to fleas and head lice which were prevalent at the time and which almost drove my mother to despair. It was an uphill struggle to keep the children clean and free from these pests as there were always 'dirty' families who did not care so much and, being so closely confined during lessons, it was impossible to prevent re-infestation.

I can remember sitting behind a boy whose family had just moved into the village. I watched in fascination the fleas swarming around his neck and the tell-tale bite marks left on his neck. I was to feel those bites in the next few days as the fleas transferred themselves to me and the others sitting close to him. When mother saw them it was off with all clothing for 'the wash', head and body thoroughly washed with carbolic coap and the stink of Jeyes Fluid sprinkled on the bedroom floor. In bed we all had to endure the gritty powder of pulverised camphor balls and the appalling stench of sulphur candles, until it seemed we had temporarily won the battle.

Of course it was not long before angry parents made the newcomers do something about their fleas, and the headmaster was soon aware of the parents' anger. Very soon we would get a visit from the 'louse nurse'. This manly built woman combed all heads over a sheet of newspaper looking for lice and worse still the nits or eggs of lice which practically welded themselves to the victim's hair. The girls with their long hair suffered worse and I can see my mother now with comb and scissors cutting out bits of infected hair from my sisters' heads which washing and combing had failed to remove. If lice or nits fell on that newspaper from the louse nurse's comb they were disposed of into the tortoise stove. The child would be given a good talking to, and some-times a box of powder to sprinkle in her hair at night. Parents of the unlucky children got a 'nurse's note' and in the worst cases a visit from the nurse, which was considered the height of humiliation.

I have mentioned pulverised camphor balls to deter fleas; we got these from the chemist in Charlbury four miles away. As father was a railway man his family was allowed to travel by rail at cheap or 'privileged' rates. It would cost 4d (or less than 2p today) to travel to Charlbury and back. Although passenger trains stopped every two hours or less, the long uphill walk from Charlbury Station to the chemist or to our doctor usually meant just missing one return train, and a long wait for another. Fourpence was a lot of money and when we got older we were often given the 4d train fare to go and collect medicines for O.A.P.s from the chemist. Often have I walked there and back just to have that money for myself or to give to mother.

Prank and punishment

At the time I had to move into the Big Room at school, to another teacher, there was talk of the coming retirement of Mr. Kinvig, who would be leaving school for good in the late summer. He had earned a good name from the village and from most of his pupils. I was not with him long enough to remember any outstanding scholastic event but I did remember seeing some-thing which will be in the memories of all those concerned for a good many years.

A gang of young boys, myself included, had been visiting the smelly stone trough by the toilets used as a urinal. We were about to walk back up the passage to the school porch and out into the playground when we found our way blocked by a mob of Big Boys. They had unscrewed the hasp of the padlock to the back door of the girls' toilets. Through this door the vaults were cleaned and cleared twice a year. This time the door was open for a prank, and unintentionally blocked the view of the porch doorway. At the bottom of the toilet block was a large heap of ashes (from the coke tortoise stoves) around which grew vicious stinging nettles five feet high. The older boys had one of the stinging nettles in their hands and were tickling the girls' bottoms with the nettle as they sat on the seats above.

We, the younger boys, saw something the older boys did not. We saw Mr. Kinvig standing in the porch doorway with his stick behind his back as he approached the open toilet vault door. When he got there we saw the stick rise and fall, and heard the shrieks as he lashed them all. He pushed the door shut and followed them back into school just as the bell for lessons went. Inside the classroom Mr. Kinvig lined up the culprits and gave them six of the best on their backsides. Some howled, some gritted their teeth and kept quiet. All knew that as soon as their fathers heard of their escapade they would get another hiding with the belt and buckle.

Fathers and teacher worked together; no-one squealed to the authorities about physical abuse, and even the culprits accepted what was given them and I don't think they held any grudge. It was life.

When the time came for Mr. and Mrs. Kinvig to retire, I remember after school walking along the pavement outside the playground when Mr. Kinvig locked the porch door for the last time. He had a number of books under his arm as he moved away, and then he saw me and came over and held out the books. 'Here, boy, take these, they may do you well in the future,' and I believe they did. That was the last I saw of him. His place was taken by a Miss Bucknell as head teacher and Miss Pratley from Lyneham as assistant teacher.

Mr. Kinvig's books remained with me until I was over sixty. They were of value although they were so old in format. The last one I gave away when I was sixty-eight; it was *Piers Ploughman*, a history of England in Saxon times. I remember the looks of disbelief on the faces of some modern children of the early eighties when I showed them my remaining books, and they made comparisons with the books they had at school.

The felling of trees

Before I progress into my teenage years I must tell of a few things which were part of my life then, and which were typical of life generally between the wars.

Those screech owls which we heard at night lived in the oak trees standing along the churchyard wall forming its boundary from our house to the village pound at its bottom. In between these oaks were several lime trees like those which form the avenue through the churchyard. The shrieks of these owls searching for food, and the ghostly white shapes of the barn owls which lived in the belfry, gave rise to the ghost stories of the churchyard at that time. The owls and the ghost stories went when the oaks were felled to provide cash for the church; the limes went at the same time including an odd lime tree much older than the rest which stood inside the churchyard by the gates, and which made our house dark. It also turned the oak gates green from the drippings from its overhanging branches and leaves.

Our churchyard is about four feet six inches above the surrounding roads, and its boundary is a flat-topped stone wall along which stood enormous chestnut trees of both red and white flowers. These were cut down in the early fifties because they were considered a danger to the houses nearby and because they blocked out the view of the church and left a lot of mess in autumn. Their destruction caused a lot of argument in the village and a lot of disappointment from those people who offered to cut them down for the firewood; they were not good burning wood, and they needed coal to make them burn well.

The villagers who dissented from the destruction of these trees were people with roots in the past and who had relatives buried in the churchyard. They were annoyed at having their relatives' graves knocked about by the felling of these giants. Both they and the trees are gone and the cottages they rented 1/6d to 6/- a week are now valued at £100,000, maybe £200,000.

Memories of the Boer War

I remember those Sundays early in my life when Dad had a lie in and got up at about 10 a.m. to have a shave and his breakfast.

We were awakened by the bells for the eight-o'clock church service, but as children we were not allowed downstairs before the adults. But we were often wide awake and we spent this time looking through a stack of Dad's Boer War magazines, one of which was entitled *With the Flag to Pretoria* and cost 3d per week. These magazines told about the battles of the Boer War, Spion Kop,

Modder River, the Siege of Ladysmith, Maggersfontein and many others. There were very few photographs except of posed portraits of the great statesmen and soldiers; all action pictures were artist's impressions and they certainly impressed my young mind. Dad would not talk about this war except to describe the Boers as very fine riders and shots. He would tell us how they all looked like old men with their beards and how they could ride a horse backwards, shoot and hit what they were aiming at.

Of course these magazines, as do most books, made out the enemy to be a vile villain while our own side was as pure as the driven snow. This we were not, and far from it, because in one instance alone we should as a nation hang our heads in shame. Any mention of concentration camps always conjures up the undisputed horrors of the Hitler regime and to a lesser degree the many other countries who have aped Hitler and his terrible camps. But to put history right, my children, I have to tell you that in the twentieth century it was us, the British, who started the vile business of concentration camps in the years between 1899 and 1901. It was we who broke up Boer families and herded them behind wire, the old men and babies, the women and young boys. Behind this wire they died in their hundreds due to deliberate neglect on our part, poor food, no sanitation beyond open pits, no medicine and no hope.

My time as a P.O.W. must have been a holiday compared with the sufferings of these civilians whose only crime was that they were Boers. It was our aim apparently to break the spirit of the Boer men who, for most of that war, showed up the many deficiencies in our army which was still being trained for the parade ground and the mass attacks of the Napoleonic Wars. Since then England had fought only one war against white men, the Crimean War, where our army was as usual totally unprepared for the conditions they were to fight under, and of the men they were to fight against. That was in 1856, yet almost fifty years on our army had learnt nothing of guerilla warfare even against the Zulus, and certainly the Boers ran rings around us until we broke them at the Modder river. Even there they had their women with them living in wretched conditions, but the Boer was a dour, persistent and valiant fighter when cornered, as he then was. It is a pity that some of that spirit had not been passed on to their descendants when they were supposed to be defending Tobruk in 1942.

My father had to march everywhere in the everlasting chase after the Boers who would not stand and fight a pitched battle, but lay in ambush and shot down our men as they, using the tactics of earlier generations, advanced in line formation against a hidden and protected enemy armed with the very best

German rifles. Over 23,000 British and Empire troops died in what was considered a minor war, and England's military reputation slumped. As Dad was marching, his legs were encased in those puttees mentioned above, and as a Guardsman the puttees had to be tightly fixed in order to look smart. On his left leg the puttee was too tight and, after marching some time in considerable pain, my father collapsed. When that puttee was removed, to use his words, 'My leg swelled like a balloon.' The varicose veins in his leg had been damaged, thus restricting the blood supply; this caused Dad to suffer a bad leg for years. His leg was not cured until he had the vein removed right up into his groin in 1938. He was off work for twelve months, being finally ready to resume work the Monday after the Second World War was declared on Sunday, September 3rd, 1939. He had in the intervening years fought through the four years and three months of the 'Great' War. Bad legs, one eye and even one hand were not regarded as impairing a man's ability to serve. Dad served until 1916 when he was demobbed from the Guards as a time serving soldier. He was conscripted back later that year under the Conscription Act, but not as a Guardsman as he was now downgraded medically. He had to serve the next two years as an instructor in the South Staffs Regiment.

Those magazines I mentioned became tatty, and some were destroyed, but in 1978 I was able to sell three, incomplete, without covers and tatty, for £25. What a fortune that stack of consecutive issues would have made.

Sunday walks

On Sunday in the better months of the year Dad would, after breakfast, take his younger children for a walk to get us out in the open air and away from mother's feet. Usually we went up Chippy Hill to the Top Road (the A361), meeting other fathers doing the same thing. They would have a natter while their children played or quarrelled around them. We would spend perhaps half an hour there counting the number of cars which passed while the fathers discussed the condition of the fields that could be seen from where we stood. Many a titbit of information not meant for young ears came my way and I sometimes got smack from Dad if later on while going home, I made the mistake of asking what Mr. So-and-so meant by what he had said.

The other walk, and more interesting to me, was Brasswell Lane, a bridle road the other side of where the Ascott road joins the Charlbury-Burford road. The verges of this lane were a mass of sloe bushes or blackthorns, with clumps of wild honeysuckle, and ancient elm trees with mounds of grey lichen on their sides on which long-tailed tits often built their well camouflaged nests.

There would be birds of all kinds nesting in these bushes and sometimes

ASCOTT UNDER WHYCHWOOD
THE ENTRANCE TO THE VILLAG

Father would pick one of us up to have a look down upon the speckled eggs or young birds in the nests. The lane and some of the sloe bushes are still there, but the farmer's pesticides and herbicides and his mechanical hedgerow trimmer have diminished that huge throng of chorus birds so that it is now quite an event to see a yellowhammer, a gold-crested wren or a long-tailed tit. Even the Jenny wrens find nesting hard as the trees with their skirts of ivy were killed by disease in the hot summer of 1976. The cuckoo is heard seldom now and has to search much further afield, as hedgerows are ripped up and the little birds who rear the cuckoo's eggs are forced further away looking for nesting sites.

This England of ours has had its countryside emasculated by the farming fraternity. Farmers ripped up hedges by the mile in order to grow more grain to increase the mountains of the stuff held in store while the Third World dies of starvation.

Those walks would end at the Sunday dinner table, where if we were lucky we would see a small piece of roast meat, roast potatoes and Yorkshire pudding. Our Yorkshire puddings would not be the airy-fairy bags of wind so beloved by many, but a thick stodgy pudding looking normal on the outside but having a thick filling. Sometimes it was baked or cooked flat a good inch thick, and then it would be spread with any jam or even sugar, and cut up for dessert.

There were always plenty of vegetables in season, and cabbage and Brussels sprouts for the winter. The humble swede (i.e. the Swedish turnip, first planted in England by John Rutherford of Melrose in 1747) was well loved, but as children we looked on cooked turnips with disdain. We preferred them raw.

Our back garden ran from the house down to the stream at the bottom. This stream started at the Vicarage Pond as overflow. The pond itself was fed from one of the village's several spring water supplies, which were piped into the village's secondhand water pipe system of the time. In fact I can remember the storage chamber being built by Mr. J. Young and the astonishing fact (to me) that two men would work through the night pumping out the water from the excavation while the concrete within was allowed to set. One of those men was Mr. Fred Dore from Leafield, one of Mr. J. Young's labourers, and he was a character in his own right.

From the pond the overflow ran via pipes and old fashioned field stone drains, down past the school, under the pavement to the corner of the green where there is now a cast iron inspection cover. From here it crosses the green towards the back of the cottage known at that time as Chance's Cottage, round past Slasher Moss's Barn and Cook's Orchard hedge, where it surfaced as a stream. This flowed past our garden to the junction with the main road where it was covered over by wooden sleepers at the point where it emerged from under the boundary wall. From these sleepers it followed the road as an open stream until just before the signal box, when it diverted under the road and railway embankment and then onwards towards the river. My father, with his mates, had to keep this under-the-railway culvert clear of rubbish; also the open stream down the middle of the Station Approach. This 'approach' was a small triangular piece of ground of about a quarter of an acre, which Dad rented and where we kept chickens. There was a similar piece of ground the other side of the crossing road, and this piece was always boggy, being used as the outlet for the rail side ditches on the up side of the line past the level crossing.

Before the river bridge was built, when there was a ford, the road into Ascott followed this boggy ground and emerged where the Churchill Arms stood as a pub until 1989. The pub is now a private house.

The open ditch in the field at the bottom of our garden, known as 'Waterloo Field', has now been filled with large hardcore and covered with soil and grass. The water still trickles its old way through the stones but the main flow has been diverted directly across the field through twelve inch pipes. The roadside ditch up to the railway has been filled in and a kerbed tarmac path has been built over it.

Where the sleepers covered the stream as it emerged under the field's boundary wall, the stream teemed with minnows, and Jenny wrens built their leaf-lined nests in the rotten holes of the sleepers. Both the minnows and the wrens were an attraction to small boys who lay on their stomachs with jam jars to catch minnows or to have a look at the wrens. Very often one of the recumbent children would feel his ankles being gripped and he would be upended into the shallow stream, getting a hiding from his parents for getting wet and making work, and also being jeered at by the bullies who had dumped him.

Birds' eggs and fag cards

As boys we collected birds' eggs, a practice now stopped by law in order to protect the diminishing number of birds in the countryside. When an egg was taken from the nest it usually meant torn clothes, muddy boots and numerous scratches and cuts to the face and hands, and often the loss of the prized trophy. In the event of the egg being saved, a hole was pricked in each end with a needle and then the egg was put to the boy's lips – whereupon he blew out the contents via the other hole. The egg was then put in a cardboard box on sawdust and usually kept under the boy's bed.

There was quite a trade in egg swapping, and rare eggs such as those of a cuckoo, a rook or a crow would command a few weeks' pocket money (usually 1d or at most 2d a week), plus a few more common eggs or cigarette cards. These latter were very fashionable and collectable at that time. A packet of ten cigarettes would contain one card while a packet of twenty contained two. These cards were very often in colour and were in sets of fifty. My first cigarette card was of a rook's nest at the top of an elm tree, from a series entitled 'Birds in the Treetops', and the cards were very informative. Complete sets of these cards today will fetch thousands of pounds and are much sought after. Smokers were always being pestered with 'Any fag cards, Guv'nor?' and would at times get very cross. Some cigarettes gave coupons which could be exchanged for scarves of knitted wool with large bands of blue or red with white bands between. Some boys would collect Player's packets and cut out the lifebelt and sailor's head, and by cutting out the background between the head and lifebelt, they were able to make a chain of Players' badges.

Large eggs such as pheasants, partridges, moorhens or plovers ('peewits' to us) were used for cooking, although the gamekeepers would give my father 2/6d for a clutch of pheasant eggs found along the line. They would not treat a small boy's pheasant eggs so generously — quite often the boy got a clout and a warning to 'leave these eggs alone or I'll call the police'. The boys soon learnt and the eggs got cooked.

My companion in birds' nesting and other adventures was usually Jack Sherborne, son of 'Chippy' Sherborne who lived across the road from us. 'Chips' Sherborne worked in my father's gang on the railway and always smoked his short-stemmed clay pipe upside down. Both Chippy and my father carried 'flag baskets' to work, holding their food and drink. These baskets were very popular at that time and were made from flat reed; they had two handles and were of the style and shape, but deeper, of a carpenter's bag. A short length of rope was passed through the handles, and the basket was hoisted on to the man's back, held there by the short cord in his hand.

My young jackdaw

Other adventures of our young days were hazel nut collecting at a notorious hedgerow called The Poplars because of the large poplars growing there and fed by the stream on the other side. Occasionally a young jackdaw would be caught at the 'Jackdaw tree', a very old dead and rotten giant whose many holes gave cover to the droves of jackdaws which nested there. This tree stood alone in the middle of a field on the way from Ascott's wooden bridge to Pudlicote. The wooden bridge crossed the river on Manor Farm ground and was the scene of much bathing and swimming, there being a hole in the river bed alleged to be fifteen feet deep.

I only ever had a young jackdaw once, and I kept it for two days in a large covered wire chick rearing run about 6' x 4' x 2' high. One day after I had put the jackdaw in the run in the open air, I heard a commotion in the elm trees ten yards away. In these trees were dozens of adult jackdaws who would dive down at the captive bird and then return to the trees. For about two hours this went on when suddenly the birds left the area and the captive. That young jackdaw died within a few hours and old men I spoke'to said, 'Ah yew, them old daws poisoned that young un, they allus does given the chance.' Well, they did not always get the chance because some of my friends had jackdaws about their homes flying free, who would settle on the boys' shoulders and take food from their hands. The death of that bird upset me and I never had a captive bird again, although mother had linnets, canaries and even bullfinches in large cages indoors at different times.

To the allotment

Whenever I came home torn and dirty, my mother would open the stair door behind the screen which stood between it and Dad in his chair with his paper. Having taken off my shoes I would creep upstairs to bed so that when

Dad looked at the clock and asked where I was, Mother could truthfully say 'He's in bed,' adding perhaps not so truthfully, 'He doesn't feel up to the mark.'

There were times, however, when Mother's patience snapped and I had to feel Dad's hand across my face or his belt and buckle on my bottom. A lot of these hidings I no doubt well deserved but there were times when Dad hit first and asked afterwards, especially if he was out of tobacco for his pipe and had no money to buy more. However, I reckon I broke even as there is no doubt that I got away with a lot I should have been belted for. 'You keep yourself from crying,' he would say as he swung his belt, 'I'll stop you from laughing.' And he did. All hidings were followed with 'and go straight up to the allotments and water the plants when you come out of school,' or we'd be given some other task up there to keep us away from the village green and the football.

Hand weeding the potatoes was a hated job and was considered worse than carrying small buckets of water from the tap below the Vicarage. 'Trinder's Tap' it was called, and we carried the water to the allotment four hundred yards away, trying to make as large a damp patch around each plant as was possible. We had to carry six buckets of water at least and a lot of this slopped over and wet our feet as we struggled uphill with it. Dad would come up after his tea and as the sun was going down over the horizon, he would say, 'Off you go to your football!' — but it would be too late: when we got to the green all the other boys would have gone home.

The allotments up the London Lane past the vicarage, or over the railway where Dad had over a quarter of an acre, were the sun around which our world made its orbit. Without allotments most village people would have starved.

Those allotments up the London Lane occupied fifty-two acres of which only four acres were used by a farmer. The rest was divided into $1/4$ acre lots with eighteen inches of grass verge between them. From Good Friday until after the potato harvest this land was a hive of industry with dozens of forks 'clack-clack-clacking' as weeds were knocked out of lumps of dug soil on its brashy ground. Men would call and shout to friends fifty yards away and the others listening to what was said would join in the laughter. There would be dozens of people there on a good evening; whole families complete with prams and wheelbarrows, and of course their dog sitting on his master's coat. They would attack the weeds and the grass on the verge taking care to save anything which the pig would eat. There would be lots of smoky fires in season as bean stalks and vines and old Brussels sprout stems or 'stoms' would be burnt. If it could be dug in for manure it was, and then there was last year's collected heap of pig manure from the sty to spread and dig in. Some people, to be independent, would push their pig muck on wheebarrows the three-quarters of a mile to their allotment rather than pay a farmer for the hire of a horse and cart; and some just because they were the type not to be beholden to any man.

During World War I when Dad was at the Front, the allotments were more valuable than ever and had to be worked by mother with what help she could get from her children: this in addition to running her home. My eldest brother Ernest, or Ern, had left school at the age of twelve to work on a farm and bring in a few coppers to the famlly purse as well as helping the war effort. As soon as a boy had reached twelve years of age and theoretically reached a certain standard of education, he was allowed to leave school.

Ernest started work on the land doing up to 10 hours a day, and after those long hours he tried his best to do what he could on the allotments. Of course the ground was not as well tended as the ground of a grown man exempt from military work, and the difference showed.

There were many exempt able-bodied men, usually farmers' sons whose fathers sat on the local Labour Boards to see who was to be exempt and who was to fight.

One day the agent for Cornbury Park Estate, who was himself an estate owner, a man by the name of Fellows, went to the allotments with his local sub-agent J. Young Senior, builder and undertaker, who lived in the village. When they came to my father's land and noticed its condition, the agent asked for the name of the plot holder. When told it was my father, he asked why he had let the allotment get into its present state. Because he is absent abroad at the war, he was told. 'In that case,' said the agent, 'he does not need the ground, take it from him and plant corn.'

When the village heard of what had happened they were outraged and sought to help mother get the ground to rights. One man, Charlie Cook's father Ben, got his horse and a borrowed plough and ploughed up the uncultivated part of Dad's piece. The other villagers helped with forks and dibbers to plant the ground so that mother's family kept this allotment and were provided with food. I thank those long dead Ascott people for their kindness. Those so-called gentry were no different from those who, much less than a hundred years earlier, were hanging boys of nine years of age for the theft of five shillings! Those villagers who had 40/- and thus were entitled to the vote changed from Tory to Liberal and many stayed that way for good.

Fanny Rathband, née Honeyborn, who died in 1939 in Chipping Norton workhouse, the last surviving Ascott martyr and, in 1873, the youngest martyr at 16.

The Ascott Martyrs

This also strengthened the anti-Tory vote in Dad's family, and also those of his brothers. Their mother, my grandmother, was one of the crowd of Ascott women who demonstrated against Robert Hambidge, of Crown Farm, in 1873 for employing two Ramsden men to do the work that should have been done by his own men then on strike for better wages.

Sixteen Ascott women, today known as the Ascott Martyrs, were sent to prison with hard labour for ten days for daring to support their locked-out farmworker men folk. Seven of the sixteen were of my family tree, including my grandmother's sister-in-law, Jane Honeybone, who married my grandfather's brother Robert.

There were two clergymen on the magistrates' bench at Chipping Norton; these men were called 'squaresons', a cross between a squire and a parson. The upshot of the affair was that there was a public outcry against sending these women to prison, two of whom had babies at their breasts. Extra police were drafted in and the newspapers took up the matter. The feeling was intense and petitions for the immediate release of the women were sent to the Home Office. Subscriptions of £80 (a very large sum in the days of 9/- a week wages) came in from the country people, and on their release the sixteen women were presented with £5 apiece from the Agricultural Workers Union. In front of Crown Farm, the home of the farmer concerned, Joseph Arch – the founder of the National Union of Agricultural Workers – gave the women their £5 each. Each got Queen Victoria's pardon (too late, as they had served their sentence) and a florin (or two shillings) each. They also received a blanket or a petticoat each, but there is a dispute as to which it was.

It was the end of parsons sitting as magistrates. This story can be read in full in Joseph Arch's autobiography (*From Ploughtail to Parliament*, from The Crescent Library).

The martyrs' names were displayed on an eight-sided seat around a horse chestnut tree planted on the village green in their honour. The seat was paid for by a local Tory farmer, Ivor Warner, whose wife, Doris White's mother, was a Moss before marriage. The seat has 16 names on its octagonal sides, and surrounds a strapping young chestnut tree on the village green.

My grandmother's name was Hannah Moss, and I have dim memories of her putting butter on my badly sun-blistered arms, standing outside her front door on the path lined with eighteen-inch high box hedging. Box has a scent of its own and at that time was associated with the gardens of the well-to-do. That old-world smell and the few roses around her door, her old fashioned black dress touching the ground and her almost flat black straw hat fixed to her hair with long hatpins, belong to an age long past. The quietness of the village with its wealth of smells and scents, the squawking of its chickens running free range, and those clouds of butterflies, are a picture of a summer's day in Ascott village when everyone knew everyone; and family ties were very strong.

A life-saving medal and the problem of floods

My grandfather, Walter Moss, won a life-saving medal for saving a man whose pony and trap had been washed away in an exceptionally bad flood by the river bridge. Every year in my youth, this road over the level crossing, from halfway down towards the main gated entrance to Manor Farm and over the river bridge to the corners of Brickhill, was flooded. This was because of the accumulation of silt, fallen trees and reed beds in the river. This state of affairs persisted until 1937 when the Thames River Authority sent gangs of men, diggers and dredgers to remove fallen and dangerous trees and dig and dredge away the silt on which the reed beds and bulrushes flourished. It was in these rushes that the moorhens made their nests and laid the eggs gathered by hungry labourers. Swans also used these reed islands for nesting, and water rats for their hunting grounds. Occasionally there would be a flash of multi-colour as a kingfisher flew by to its nest in a bank nearby. Pike abounded in the Evenlode's waters and my brother George coming home for the weekend from St. Edward's School, Oxford, would be sure to catch one of about 6 lbs. These were gutted, cleaned and scraped, before being cut into chunks and fried, but I never really took to fresh water fish; maybe it needed a more sophisticated cook than mother, but as all she cooked got eaten I reckon she did not do too badly.

The bulrushes would grow about five feet tall and sprout a feathery top. My elder brothers and their friends would pull them up, cut off the top and roots and then run a matchstick or something a bit stronger down inside and along the whole length of the rush, pushing out the white pithy centre. With this they made rosettes of many designs for their lapels. These looked wonderful when first fixed to the coat, but a few hours in the open air and sunlight would discolour them until they went brown and were discarded.

My brother George was a crack shot with a catapult, and I have seen him hit a matchstick stuck in the end of a broken bulrush near this river bridge on one of those Sunday mornings.

'Pitch and Toss' was a game played by the youth of Ascott on a Sunday morning. Though we were told it was illegal, this game was often played in

Left to right: Bob Storey, Fred Dore (of Leafield) and Michael Shayler (Bob's brother-in-law).

the 'Brickhill' next to the river bridge. It was a cross between marbles, throwing horseshoes, and darts. A stone, a washer or a button was the target and was called the mott. Players tossed coins at this mott hoping to drop one on top, when they would have won the game and the money on the ground. When this never happened the game went to the player whose coin was nearest the mott.

Alongside the road which flooded, on the right hand side going towards the bridge was a three foot high stone wall. Often in flood time a man or boy would walk along its 'toppers' and pick up the trembling rabbits crouched on it seeking refuge from the flood. Holding the rabbit by its back legs with the left hand, a short, hard cut with the edge of the right hand behind the ears would painlessly and instantly kill the animal.

Sometimes in winter time these floods would freeze and the acres of ice would be skating rinks for the hobnailed boots of boys and men. Of course there were accidents when the ice broke, but no real harm other than a soaking and a cold would result, as care was taken to keep away from the deeper flood by the river.

The other flooded exit from Ascott was at the bottom of Down Street, now called Shipton Road. To about ten yards up from the bottom corner of the left-hand cottage at the bottom of the village, the water would rise from Coldwell Brook and the river, flooding Coldwell farmyard and Meadow Lane up to the river bridge. This would be an island surrounded by water stretching to the railway line and along the lane towards Carter's Crossing. Going towards Shipton the water would reach almost to Chestnut Close entrance, and so this road too would be blocked to road traffic other than tractors, and perhaps a horse and cart. After the river dredging was completed the floods were not so deep. The only exit from Ascott was either along the railway which was forbidden, or up past the school onto London Lane, Charlbury and Leafield, and of course Burford if required.

In 1947 the village was marooned by snow-blocked roads and bread and groceries had to be brought there by train. In normal times bread and groceries and clothing etc. were brought to the village three times a week by horse van from Chipping Norton Co-op. Our house was the last one visited by this van which on Friday collected all money owing. My first job after leaving the school gates would be to hurry to the station and get Dad's wage packet so that mother could pay the Co-op. Dad's wages then were 33/6d for 44 hours, rising to 47/6d in 1938.

Mr Benfield's milk lorry

Milk in churns from the surrounding farms was despatched in the guard's van of the up trains from Ascott and was collected from the farms by Mr. Bill Benfield and his ancient, much patched and painted lorry. He would have young boys to help him load these churns at eventide, and in my turn I did likewise, but his surly temper when he was late (which was often) and his very infrequent payment for my labour made me fight shy of his work offers.

Mr. Benfield was one of a family of butchers from Leafield who had fought in the Yeomanry in the First World War, as he had at the time owned his own horse, this being essential for entry into the Yeomanry.

He was a short man who always wore brown leather gaiters and shoes when he was going socialising at night, and he was always whistling between his teeth — more of a hiss than a whistle.

His lorry was a joke for miles around the village. He had adapted a 30 cwt Bedford for his business of haulier, and the vehicle could be adapted for cattle transport after a half-hour's work by two men fitting tall side rails of metal struts and wooden spars and a long rear tailgate which acted as a loading ramp for animals.

Bill was always falling foul of the Ministry of Transport inspector, and before each market day he would be seen trying to put right all those items reported earlier by the inspector. When I was fourteen I helped to rebuild this vehicle and the result would have given pleasure to Heath Robinson, as Bill would not buy bolts of the right length. He always bought them too long which meant fitting them with wooden blocks and metal washers before the nuts could be tightened. When not cattle hauling Bill would haul coal from Shipton station to the gas works, which then was situated at the entrance to Shipton from the Ascott road. It is gone now and an old people's home called Bowerham stands on its site.

From the gas works Mr. Benfield would collect coke and tar for local customers. Churches and schools were his customers for coke. Farmers used the tar for waterproofing their buildings. At what should have been precise times of the day Mr. Benfield was supposed to deliver churns of milk from local farmers to Ascott station. Irate train guards, fed up with waiting for him to arrive, would send their trains on their way and Bill would get to the station often to see the tail lights of the train disappearing under Coopers Bridge. Bill lost that contract and the milk was collected by tankers.

(In those days cows were not tuberculin tested, and many were afflicted by 'consumption'. This affected the milk and, since the cows were hand milked amid their manure, their milk was not as good as it is today. There was no washing of cows' udders or teats, or of the hands of the milkers. Often when passing a cow being milked I would see brown spots in the bucket showing where dirt was being washed into it by the milk. My brother Ern, then a farm worker, would never have milk in any shape or form — he had seen enough.)

Mr. Benfield's depot was that yard next to our neighbour's house and called Moss's Yard because Slasher Moss rented it and kept his horse, hay and cart there. Since I was living so near I was always trying to avoid Mr. Benfield and his 'Half a minute, young 'un, giss a bit of a hand'.

After World War II, having built my own home, I was trying to build up a small builder's business, and as I had no transport other than my cycle I had to keep the right side of Bill in order to get my equipment moved. Bill took advantage of this and was always at my door asking for a 'drop of paint — just a jam jar full'. Well, at 12/6d a gallon that jam jar of paint cost me 1/7d, equal to an hour's wages at that time. All I got from Benfield was 'I'll see tha', but I suppose it was as broad as it was long as he never charged me a lot for what he did for me.

Poor old Bill died about 1960 in the stables where Slasher once kept his horse. He had been kicked out of his lodgings at Jack Honeybone's (more of him later), and he had lived rough in these stables. Poor food and pneumonia killed him; his passing leaving another gap he had filled as a 'character' in the village.

Slasher Moss

As we have mentioned Slasher Moss several times, perhaps I should tell you a bit more about him. He got his name Slasher from his threats to young boys trying to wind him up, that he would 'put his whipcord across their backs'.

A distant relative of my father, he had been one of the village stalwarts in his time and had helped physically to throw off the village green some Gypsies who had camped there and then refused to move. 'Old Thomas' had been 'Old Thomas' for as long as I could remember. He used his yard for his business of haulier or carter, but he was a loner, although he was married and had two daughters. Nellie (mentioned elsewhere) was working for Mr. Kinvig, and we called her Ginny — but I reckon that was short for some other name. In any case she was a married women, a Mrs. Hudson, whose husband had deserted her.

Thomas's father had owned six shire horses which were stabled in that gap between the row of houses facing the church clock. His trade was hauling timber from the Forest down into Ascott to the sawpits situated where there is now a stone, blue slated pair of semi-detached cottages, built in 1899, next to the 'school house'. At the pits (which were stone lined, long holes about three feet wide, eight to ten feet lonf and six feet deep), the logs would be placed on cross timbers over the hole and chocked firm and still. A line would be 'popped' along the top to mark the first cut. This was done by dipping a string into almost anything — lime, chalk, flour, paint — and offering it over the place to be sawn. It would be held down tight at the ends of the tree and then twanged or popped like a bowstring. This left a line visible to the man standing on the tree with a long two-handled saw, one end of which he fed into the pit to his mate standing under the tree. With the man at the top, who got more money, guiding the saw along the line, and the man underneath pulling the saw down, the tree would be cut up for timber.

As the forest receded from the village locality, the timber was cut up at Cornbury Estate sawmills in the Forest about the turn of the century.

With the decline in the timber hauling business and the death of his father, young Tom — as he was then — got his living as a carter hauling coal and animal feed to the villages in the locality until the arrival of the motor vehicle cut this work down in the village area.

With both daughters at work, Thomas had himself and his wife to keep and somehow he managed that with his cart and an old horse. Old horses they were too; I can remember the vet with a hammer and cold chisel knocking off about half an inch from the tops of one horse's bottom teeth, and then using a large shoeing rasp to file them down level so that the horse could eat better. (Hence the expression 'too long in the tooth' for age.) All the while that horse was held still by a 'twitch', which was a loop of leather about three-eighths of an inch wide, making a loop about fist-sized, fixed to a short wood handle. This loop of leather thong was put around the horse's top lip and twisted tight by the wood handle. That way a horse's head was kept still for a vet to work. I knew of two of Slasher's horses who dropped dead in their shafts through old age and, I suspect, under-feeding.

Old Tom wore off-white corduroy trousers 'yorked', that is tied with a leather strap under the knee. This kept his trouser bottoms out of the mud and I suspect held any coins which might escape through holes in his pockets. He wore a tunic or jacket in the style of the 1880s, and his peaked 'drover's cap' belonged to that era too.

Thomas, like the rest of the men, had a large allotment on which he grew barley for his pig, a few oats for his horse and vegetables for his family. Often we would hear him from our house cutting chaff for his horse using the chaff cutter fixed in the loft over his horse cart. This 'chaff' was not the 'kevins' from the threshing drum but a mixture of straw and hay laid in the trough of the chaff cutter. This was fed through the blades by the left hand as the right hand turned the wheel holding the blades by the handle fixed to the rim of this wheel. The cutter made a noise of 'chiff-chaff-chiff-chaff' and so on for about three minutes, by which time Thomas considered he had enough, with a handful of oats, to feed his horse. For some time Thomas would lean on the bottom half of the stable door and watch his horse eat. Very often we would hear him say, 'Git up there, dun't yut so fast', as the hungry horse made short work of his supper.

Thomas had a small beehive-shaped rick of hay in his yard, made from grass cut from the churchyard and from the roadside verges. On bonfire nights he would stand near this rick watching the fire and the fireworks in case any part of these set his precious hay alight. He went home when the fire was out. I have wondered if he ever suspected that someone was removing hay from this rick, because someone did. Harry Cook, Charlie's son, and myself would often go to the rick, as soon as Thomas was safely away, and pull out armfuls of hay from the sides so as not to leave a hole; we fed it to the horse who seemed to welcome our visits and voices.

Water for this horse had to be carried a hundred yards from a standpipe by the village green. Between our cottages there was a well whence most of the water for the house came. It was about twelve feet deep, and water was pulled up in a bucket by means of a 'well hook' or 'welluk'. This was a ten-foot pole with a spring clip jaw at one end. Sometimes we lost a bucket and had to fish for it with a hook tied on a piece of string. Our use of this well was not always appreciated by C. Cook senior who would make disparaging remarks to us children, not to Dad, that he was 'the only bugger to clean out the well'.

One day we were talking about a grave being flooded before a funeral when it dawned on us that the churchyard must be draining into our well. Thereafter we got our water from the tap by the green until 1953, when I piped it into mother's house, gave her a sink and an extra window to the back room, and thus made her life a little more tolerable. I had bought the cottage from Cornbury Park Estate for £200 in 1952 for her and Dad. I also laid on drains and put in a septic tank.

Helping Frank Longshaw, the blacksmith

Thomas worked hand in glove with Mr. Frank Longshaw from Shipton who ran the coal and animal feed wharf for Marriots Ltd at Ascott station yard. They spent a lot of time chatting while Thomas waited for a customer without transport to arrive for coal who would ask him to deliver it. When Thomas lost his last horse he sold his cart and bought a box on wheels with which he would deliver a cwt of coal anywhere in the village for 3d. This could include walking two miles or more there and back. In the evenings Thomas gave the blacksmith a hand with a sledge hammer, if Mr. Andrews was making 'drugs': these were iron shoes to put under waggon wheels to be chained on to steady the waggon downhill by locking the rear wheels. The drug acted as an iron sledge and sparks flew like fireworks if the waggon was heavily loaded. This sledge prevented the waggons from over-running the horses which were also leaning backwards on their legs to help hold back the waggon.

The three-quarter inch thick lump of iron would be white hot when the blacksmith withdrew it from the fire and held it on the anvil. He would hit it in a spot with his shoe-making hammer, and Thomas would bring his sledge down on that spot with a 'tump': soon both hammers would be going so fast that all one heard was a 'tump-tum-tump-tum-tump-tum' as sledgehammer made the tump while the smaller hammer made the tum. Sometimes when the huge iron tyres or rims of a waggon's wooden wheels were being made, Thomas would give a hand with the sledge when the metal was spliced with a fire weld-joint.

For these labours Thomas received a few coppers which he carefully put in a dirty black bag tied at the neck, which he pulled from his pocket. The old men of that time were careful with their money and I have seen my dad put the flat of his hand in his back pocket, fingers first, and then let the money in his palm, held there by his thumb, slowly fall into the pocket. Dad once told his family, at tea, of the time he joined the Grenadier Guards and how he guarded his money by keeping his hand on it. I asked 'How much was it?', and he replied '1$^{1}/_{2}$d old money'. In 1896 that was almost two hours work for a farm labourer.

In 1940 Thomas Moss collapsed and died in his yard, being found by my mother. His daughters and son lived on for another twenty years or more. His descendants live at Leafield today.

In the fifties I remember sharpening a saw for one of Tom's daughters. Now cottage saws were no fun to sharpen as they usually had been badly mis-sharpened by the cottager who had also worn off the set to the teeth. The going rate at that time for 'touching up' a reasonably maintained saw was 2/6d, as saw files at that time cost 4/6d and would not do many saws if they were in bad condition. Because I knew these two Moss ladies I decided to charge them 6d as I knew they were poor. When I said, 'Sixpence, please,' I can still see the look of horror in their faces. 'Sixpence,' one said. 'We work all day for that.' Now knowing others in the village and elsewhere who were still getting Victorian wages because they were old and would not, for fear of eviction from their tied cottages, ask for more, then I do not doubt that what the women said was true. As I knew their employers to be dyed-in-the-wool Tories, I am sure they were speaking the truth.

'They'll find out, they allus does'

In 1946 my Uncle William would call in when I was building my house and help move a few bricks or break a few stones for hard core, but he stopped coming. As I liked his company and his help I asked him next time we met why he had stopped. He said, 'My boy, I'm living on Lloyd George's pension (ten shillings I believe it was then), and someone has shopped me for working for you, so I can't come any more.' Even though I promised to deny that I had given him money and would say that he was working as a wedding present for me, he would not budge. 'They'll find out, they allus does,' he said. This was also the answer he gave when I asked him why he had not voted at the last election. As a canvasser I knew his sympathies, and I tried to make sure that all who thought as I did, turned up on the day of the election. 'They' — by which he meant the bosses — 'will find out, and turn us out, so we don't vote.' But those same bosses could come unstuck... as they did with my father.

In the days just after World War I when only Tories and Liberals fought for local seats in the shires, those people who were anti-Tory voted Liberal whether or not they were Liberal sympathisers. Farmer Hambidge, the son of the Hambidge involved in the Ascott Martyrs affair, was a noted Tory and tight with his money. At election time, however, he, like others of his ilk, could find the money to bribe his workers and others with beer so long as they promised to vote for the 'right party', *his* party.

It was the custom then, as it had been for years before, for elections to be occasions of open bribery, and Hambidge was no different from any other boss. The usual threat or advice was always given: 'We shall know which way you vote, we can find out,' and of course many believed this and those who did not either voted for his party to be sure, or abstained.

Now on this occasion Hambidge was taking a load of voters to Shipton-under-Wychwood polling station in his waggon and horses, when they stopped at the Churchill Arms for the first free drink and bribe of the morning. Pubs were open all day, and election days were something of an outing for those workers (no women) who were independent enough to please themselves whether they voted or not. Unfortunately there were few such men, as most men were tied to the bosses who owned their tied cottages, and when the boss said 'Vote!' they voted. Well now, on this day as Hambidge bought his workers their free beer, and harangued them as to their duty to be done at the poll, my father walked into the pub for a drink on his way to vote. As he was friendly with Hambidge's men, he joined in their conversation, and as Hambidge handed out the pints for his men, one or two of them said, 'Guvnor, what about old Ern here, he's one of us?' 'No,' said Hambidge, 'he's a damn Liberal.'

And so Dad bought his own drink.

After the men had finished their beer Hambidge took them to the Red Horse pub at Shipton-under-Wychwood, within two hundred yards of the polling station at the school. Here Hambidge gave the men their final orders and beer just as Dad, who had left the Churchill Arms earlier and walked along the railway to Shipton, walked in. Again the men asked Hambidge, 'What about old Ern?' and again Hambidge said, 'No beer for a damn Liberal.' At this the men whispered amongst themselves and, with Hambidge's final exhortation to vote for the 'right party' and 'I shall know how you vote, mind', the men went off to vote.

With the voting over, the men returned to the Red Horse for a final drink and a debrief by Hambidge. With his beer in their hands, Hambidge said 'Well, did you vote for-the right party?' 'Yes, Guvnor, we did, we voted Liberal because of how you treated old Ern,' and the men stayed at the pub and made a day of it, while a fuming Hambidge went home alone. Many men were employed on farms those days and Hambidge dare not evict all his men as punishment, with harvest due, so he had to grin and bear it.

Some days later, Dad was digging his allotments 'over the line' by the railway, using a fork whose handle was painted bright red. It was red because that was the only paint Dad could beg off the painters who came occasionally to paint signal gantries etc., but at that time it was the political colour of the Liberals. Hambidge was walking by on his way to see his sister, Mrs. Chaundy, at Manor Farm, when he saw Dad. As Dad straightened his back to say 'Good day Guvnor', Hambidge spotted the fork. 'Damme Moss! You have even got a damn Liberal fork.' 'Yes, Guvnor, and a Liberal spade and vote too.' Dad was safe, he did not work for Hambidge or 'Phee Whit' as people called him behind his back. Hambidge's squeaky voice was so reminiscent of the 'peewit', or plover, which haunted the meadows in great flocks. Plovers searched for the liver flukes which clung to the grass waiting to be eaten by sheep and then in their turn eat the sheep's livers. In time 'Phee Whit' Hambidge was shortened to 'Squeaker' and this stuck until his death in the fifties.

Going for slack

One of my jobs as a nine-year-old was to push our margarine box on pram wheels up to the station yard to Mr. Frank Longshaw's hut, either for 6d worth of coal, or 'slack', or for barley meal for our pig. My younger brother and sister came along to help push as it was all uphill to the station. Sometimes we got bran for the rabbit, and Mr. Longshaw was usually generous to us and gave us a little extra. We loved the floury smell of that hut, stacked with sacks of corn or barley meal, and heated by a little tortoise stove. I seem to remember a grey tabby and white cat drinking milk from a saucer at his feet on one occasion. I expect it was a cat from the nearby pub.

Mr. Longshaw had a terrier dog with him to kill the rats which abounded under his hut and deep into the rail embankment. Most of the sacks in that hut had rat holes in them stuffed with hay which stopped the corn falling out. There would be corn and flour on the floor each morning, which Mr. Longshaw swept up and put in a sack. Sometimes he would give us some of this for our chickens as it was soiled with dirt and rat droppings.

Outside the hut a number of sticks about four feet long would be stuck into the ground at one end, while the other was bent over with a wire, with a noose on the other end. This noose would be fixed to guard a rat run and was triggered by a rat going through it. Most mornings would see three or four rats hanging with the noose around their necks from the stick which had now sprung upright.

Frank and his hut are long gone now, missed by my generation or such of us who are left and can remember him. He has joined that long list of Ascott men who made Ascott a compact rural village so different from the dormitory it now is. Coal fires generally are a thing of the past, and late autumn and winter days are not now made worse by the clouds of evil smelling chimney smoke beaten down the roofs and into a person's face by the windy weather of the times. I suppose that is one blessing, together with the absence of smog for which we can now be thankful. Smog was a killer, utterly depressing with its damp mass blocking out God's sunlight for days at a time if there was no wind. Smog was a mixture of fog and smoke, the sulphurous content of which damaged the lungs of human beings, and I have no doubt of animals too. At one period after the Second World War, I believe it was in the late forties or early fifties, we had smog over most of England for longer than three weeks, when every dreary day seemed like night turned white. This smog killed many tens of thousands of old and sick people, and led to the Clean Air Act, which prohibited the burning of open fires and coal in certain areas. Liquid gas at first gradually gave way to natural gas and oil which, with the electricity always available after its arrival around 1933, made living a lot easier, cleaner and healthier.

Milk deliveries

Milk for the home came each morning and afternoon from a man with a small churn fixed on iron wheels with tin dippers or measures hanging by their handles from its top. This type of delivery was cut to once a day as the man was either the publican of the Swan public house, Mr. 'Nobby' Clarke, or a farmer; and two deliveries were proving uneconomical. For years the milk was brought to our door by Miss Pearse, a farmer's daughter, who lived at Coldwell Farm after the Ashbys left it. When, after many years, Miss Pearse left to get married, the milk business was taken over by Reg Barrett, son-in-law of Tom Chaundy of Yew Tree Farm, Ascott. Reg Barrett was not an Ascott man; he married into Ascott and used Parkes the Heggler's old van to deliver the milk. Progress was catching up with the times at last. Milk was now pasteurised, cooled and bottled. No longer did we have that warm frothy mix of fresh milk but cool bottles left at the doorstep while most of us were asleep. This point was appreciated by tomtits who tore off the paper plug to the bottle top and pecked at the cream congealing on top of the milk.

The Pearse family now have a farm, farmhouse and yard on the hillside over the railway, and in line with Lyneham Clump. There is also a bungalow for one of the sons built where the old red brick barn stood until the late forties.

A working lunch

I must mention the term 'thumb piece' widely used in the past to describe a labourer's lunch eaten under a hedgerow. His drink would be, most often, a bottle of milkless unsweetened tea or sometimes, in my Dad's case, unmilked or very sweet cold tea. His food was often the top of a cottage loaf cut in half, spread with margarine or pig's lard or dripping, and a wedge of 'rat trap' cheese or a chunk of fat bacon. All working men carried large 'shut knives' or pocket knives for the multitude of jobs for which a knife was necessary — including cutting up their lunch. They would cut a chunk of bread, holding it on the blade with the thumb which had held the bread steady while being cut, and carry this to the mouth, knife as well. This was followed by a piece of cheese or, if fat bacon was on the menu, bread and bacon were cut at the same time and eaten as above. The knife was always drawn through the food towards the thumb. Large onions with the outer skin peeled off were eaten like apples, and were much appreciated. Spanish onions were coveted but it was years before they, the cheese and bread were sliced and put together in sandwich form.

The man would sit with a two and a half hundredweight size Hudson sack or an old coat around his shoulders to keep out the cold. These sacks (the manufacturer's name, Hudson, was stencilled on the side) were very large and strongly woven, and made ideal cover against rain and snow for head, shoulders and back.

While he ate his lunch at the headland under the lee of a hedgerow, his horses would be eating from their nose-bags. These were specially made bags to put over the horse's mouth and part of his face, and were fixed around the neck. They would contain oats mixed with chaff-cutter hay in small pieces, or some cracked maize (as Indian Corn was called). A good carter looked after his horses and tried to get the best feed he could for them, as he knew that the better fed animals lived longer and worked harder. He would even steal food for them.

Dad's lunches were no different from those of other labourers. Sometimes cold vegetables, left-overs from yesterday's meals, would be put in a basin and covered with a cloth as a little change from the everlasting bread, cheese and fat bacon. Although quite a lot of jam was made by labourers' families it was not welcomed in a working lunch as it was regarded as 'kiddies' pap, yunt got no feed to ut'. But strangely a small jam turnover would be appreciated, perhaps for the baked pastry around the jam.

When Dad came home from work there would be a rush to open his basket. If Dad was smiling when he put his bag down, we guessed there was something special inside. Often it was a rabbit, a hare, partridge or pheasant, or even mushrooms — very welcome except by the youngster detailed to 'feather' that bird or gut that rabbit or hare. These 'guts' went to the ferrets. It was the odds and ends of crusts and more particularly the bottle which the children were searching for. Somehow these crusts tasted better than the fresh bread given by mother, and the cold sweet tea tasted like nectar. We made sure that each one had his turn at the bottle by allowing it to one person in turn each day.

When Dad found hazel nuts along the line he might put some in his bag but usually he kept them in his pockets. He would pull out both closed hands at the same time and offer his fists first to my sister and say, 'Which hand has it?' and she would tap one fist. If she was right, she had the nuts; if she was wrong, they went back into the pockets to be withdrawn again and offered to the next child. As Dad put nuts in both pockets it was a job to decide which fist was going to hold the nuts, but somehow we all got some.

The crystal set

My brothers and sisters often remarked on the Christmas when a crystal wireless set was purchased for £1.1.0d, and a pair of headphones for £1. After much twiddling of the knob while holding the fine spring-like wire called the cat's whisker against the crystal, music and voices could be heard by the lucky one with the headphones. This led to arguments only halved when the headphones were split into the two earpieces and used as two receivers. It was a novelty for a while; it put us in the social scale above those without. When brother Olave fixed a wire up into Dad's bedroom and he was able to listen in while in bed, we thought we really had arrived at the summit. However, it was not long before the novelty wore off and we even came to hate that crystal set as we were always being told to be quiet and threatened with a clout if we spoke or made a noise. We children were glad sometimes to go to bed 'out of the way'.

One day we noticed Dad carrying a large wooden box home from the station. We could see that it was shut all round and must be heavy with something because Dad put it on the road and rolled it for a distance before again picking it up. That night we were sent to bed early and, as it was not raining, we sat up in bed listening to the sound of nails being withdrawn as the box was opened.

Soon the sound of music was heard — I think it was 'The Laughing Policeman'. We crept out of bed and down the stairs the better to hear, but we stayed on the stairs behind the doors. Song after song we heard with a few hymns like 'Nearer my God to Thee'; and Harry Lauder and the march 'Liberty Bell'. We could not restrain ourselves and in our excitement we forced open the door to Dad's shout of 'Go back to bed, you can see it tomorrow'. Then Mother said, 'Let them stay awhile Ern, and they will sleep better afterwards'. So we were allowed into the front room and saw for the first time a wind-up gramophone with a large funnel-like horn on top and a black round thing spinning around on top of the box. It was luxury; we were as good as the rest, and Mother, who had scraped and saved to buy this wonder and thirty records for fifty shillings without saying anything, was as happy as I have ever seen her. She was glad that her family was happy and now she could have music while she worked. New records of up-to-date tunes could be bought in Woolworths, Oxford, for sixpence. That we had to go short of sweets for a while we did not mind, and always raced home from school to put a record on the gramophone.

In due course, after the arrival of electricity during the thirties, we, or rather Mother, bought a 'loud speaker' wireless set and life took on a different dimension. Of course this loud speaker had its drawbacks. News time was sacred and no one must fidget or speak, especially if the accumulators were running flat. Then there was misery until we got it recharged. This meant us going without for a few days as the recharge was done in the next village and we had to wait until we found someone going there. Soon we found the money to buy a spare so that we never lost the use of the set. However, as we could get more than one station and some of them foreign, like Luxemburg, there were always arguments as to what we should have on. Dad always won but as he was no good mechanically, he would order one of us, usually me, to get the station and I had to tune it in for him. This state of affairs lasted until just before I joined the R.A.F., when I bought Mother a mains set for £10 — nearly three weeks' wages. It was a Burgorne, the height of luxury, and lasted almost ten years.

At Mr. Andrews' forge

The forge, or blacksmith's as it was sometimes called, was about a hundred yards from our cottage. It is a garage for car repairs now, but in our early days, on coming home from school, we would take a peek inside at the white hot metal being formed into horseshoes or other interesting items.

When the noise of many children around his door caused the blacksmith to shoo most of the children away, he would sometimes let me stay. I pumped his bellows via the long wooden handle with its white cow horn on the end and held the long lengths of horseshoe iron which he cut off to lengths. This he did by placing the metal on a bit of old three-cornered file that had been de-tempered by heating it and allowing it to cool, and then striking the bar directly over this file with his sledge hammer. This blow would cut the bar half-way through, so it was turned over to be treated as before to complete the job. If the metal was not held just right, a shock would go up my arms and my palms would sting like the devil for some time afterwards.

As I grew older I spent quite a bit of my spare time in the forge and received perhaps 2d a week for my help. It was then possible to buy quite a few sweets with ^{1}/2d, approximately worth one-fifth of a penny today.

Mr. James Andrews was the blacksmith, and as I remember him, smartened up with his trilby hat slightly back on his head and a pint cup of beer to his lips, he reminded me of that advert of the times for Bulmers Cider. Even the twinkle in his eye had the same gleam as the eyes of the rustic gentleman in the advert. He rode a B.S.A. motor cycle with sidecar in which he carried his tools when he went away to shoe the horses of farmers who would not bring them to his shoeing shop, and also when he went to farms to ring young pigs or old ones who had lost their nose ring.

The art of ringing pigs

Pigs were ringed to stop them rooting up the floors of their sties or the fields in which they were allowed to roam. Unrung pigs will turn a meadow into a ploughed field in no time as they root for food under the turf. Pigs will eat almost anything and will certainly kill large trees by eating the bark off the base of the trunk.

To ring the pig, bought copper or brass rings made like a split ring would be used, if the customer preferred and could pay. Otherwise pig rings would be made from small horseshoe nails with the head heated and flattened to the size of a shilling and with the pointed end intact. These flattened nails would be curved into a half circle before leaving the smithy. On arriving at the farm the pig would be caught and held by the farmer or one of his men, and the blacksmith would insert one of his flattened nails into a special pair of tongs which he placed over the ridge round the pig's nostrils at the top and then squeezed tight. The tongs would force the ring into a circle after the point had penetrated the gristle of the nose. The point was squeezed tight under the flattened head and the job was done. There would be squeals of course, and maybe a spot of blood, but the pig had forgotten its ordeal by next meal time.

I had many rides in that sidecar until the engine of the cycle had got so worn it had to be scrapped. The sidecar was sold and pig ringing outside the village was left to the vets.

Most of the blacksmith's tools were home made and in the stone water trough next to the fire were many tongs with differently shaped jaws, usually made from old shoeing rasps because of their superior steel. The different shapes of the tongs' jaws allowed the blacksmith to position heated metal in the right position for shaping without having to stop and move the tongs around to get another grip. With the tongs would be many different sized pritchells and punches, together with a collection of chisels. There were also many peculiar shaped lumps of metal clamped in the jaws of strong wire handles. These were used to form different patterns on hot metal when struck with a heavy hammer. When I was twelve I was allowed to finish a new horse-shoe that had been scrapped because of a fault in the 'Belgian rubbish' — which was what the blacksmith called that particular piece of metal.

I formed the unfinished side to the correct shape, punched the seven holes, four on one side, three on the other, with the special tool that formed the proper recess for the nail head, and punched out the rest of the nail hole with a pritchell. I then made the toe clips and one side clip to complete the job. The blacksmith looked at it, grunted, and said, 'I suppose it's not too bad for a boy, but it took a long time and coke costs money' — with that he threw it on the scrap heap.

The notices of forthcoming village events and meetings were posted on an ancient dilapidated board to the side of the entrance door to the blacksmith's shop. It was against the front and side of this shop that farm implements, repaired and awaiting repair, were placed. The blacksmith also kept a lot of Sussex chickens which rooted around his yard and especially in the shoeing shop, eating the flakes of rasped hoof which lay white on the floor.

It was about this time in the early thirties that oxyacetylene came to the blacksmith's shop, and he started welding joints he would otherwise have had to forge, weld or join by nuts and bolts or rivets. The acetylene was made in the shoeing shop from lumps of carbide which looked like pieces of broken stone but which, when water was added, produced heat and gas. This gas was in a separate container floating in a tank of water and was added to the oxygen via a system of rubber pipes and brass valves. The oxygen was kept in a tall cylinder with valves and gauges at its top. The mixture was fed to the torch by rubber tubes and when lit this torch gave off an adjustable flame of terrific heat which could be used for joining or cutting metals. Obviously this welding was not done when horses were there. One day the acetylene tank burst and blew the stone roof off one side of the shoeing shop.

The carbide which was used for welding was also used to fuel headlights for cars, motorcycles and portable lights, and gave a much brighter and bigger light than the glimmer from oil lamps. Carbide for cycle lamps could be bought in twelve inch long round tins for 1/3d from Mr. 'Puffer' Willis, the harness maker and cycle repair man of Shipton-under-Wychwood.

Loutish pranks

Unfortunately carbide could also be used for other things, such as loutish pranks. If one could get hold of a screw stopper bottle or a surplus carbide tin (the bottles were usually on deposit and returnable), and a knob of carbide, one could cause a very loud and frightening bang a few minutes after the water and carbide in the bottle had been added and the stopper screwed up tight or the lid stamped tight. The extent of the bang and the delay before it occurred depended upon the strength of the container, the size of the carbide knob, the amount of water, and how well the container was closed. The loaded container would be placed by the victim's door or on a window ledge while the louts ran to a place of concealment to watch.

When the pressure of the gas could not be contained any longer it would explode and break the window glass if placed close enough. It certainly brought a very irate householder to the door with a mob of crying or excited children. When one lout had an eye damaged by the explosion of a container he had held onto too long, the practice of playing with carbide and water ceased as parents monitored the possession of the carbide, and made sure it was only used for the right purpose. Spent carbide was an evil smelling whitish paste hard to dispose of in the days before dustcart collections.

The blacksmith had started to sell petrol in one-gallon B.P. tins to the several motor cyclists and the three 'Ford T' car owners in the village, but regulations came into force regarding the storage and retailing of petrol, and he had to give up. This was just as well as there were white hot sparks everywhere in that shop, and it would not have been long before an accident occurred. Outside his door he had a large blue enamelled advertisement for B.P. petrol, and this gave us a feeling of change in the air for the village. Advertising plates seemed to indicate progress only seen in towns and town shops.

Shoeing horses

Horseshoeing was fascinating to me as a boy but was a stinking, smoky job that was sometimes brutal. When the horse to be shod was brought into the stable the person bringing it usually stood at its head and talked soothingly to it if it was of a nervous type; otherwise the horse would be tied to a ring in the empty hay rack. The blacksmith knew most of the horses for miles around and, as I pumped the bellows in the evening, a farmer or his man would call and ask when he could bring 'Old Tom' or 'Bruin' or 'Nelly' to be re-shod. The blacksmith would ask, 'All round?' — meaning a complete set of shoes — and the man would tell him. Later that evening the blacksmith cut the metal for the shoes as he seemed to carry the size of the horses' feet in his head. He never referred to any paper, and when he made the shoes very little adjustment was required. I thought it was marvellous as there were so many different sizes to remember.

The blacksmith would put his box of tools close to the leg of the horse he was going to reshoe, and, picking up the foot by that tuft of hair shire horses had around their feet, he would stand back to back with the horse and put the foot between his legs. He held the horse's leg tight with his own thigh while a pair of tongs was used to loosen the shoe and finally remove it. He would then roughly clean the hoof and trim off any surplus hoof that had grown too long. The shoe for that foot would have been warming up on the fire and would be collected (when first put on the anvil) by hammering a pritchell into a nail hole and so it was carried to the horse. The foot was picked up as before and the hot shoe placed on it tightly to burn a bed for the shoe in the hoof. The smoke and smell was awful; sometimes a nervous horse would shy and prance around and the angry blacksmith would give it a clout with his hammer which made the horse worse.

A lot of stroking and soothing words were required before the blacksmith could fit the shoe he had cooled in the water trough by his fire. With a final check to see that the shoe fitted, the blacksmith would put four nails head first into his mouth, one other between his left thumb and forefinger, grasped by the head, and the other two in the palm of that left hand and secured by closed fingers.

Keeping the shoe still by holding his left hand fist-like against it, he would put the nail he held between his thumb and finger into the first hole, leaning the head slightly towards the centre of the hoof. He would then hammer home the nail tight and with the forked claw of his hammer would twist the surplus nail point off leaving a small piece of the nail showing. Another check to see that the shoe had not moved, and the blacksmith would then hammer in the remaining nails leaning the heads as before until he had them all fixed. He then put the closed jaws of his tongs under the broken end of the nail and gave its head a good clout with his hammer. This bent outwards the tiny three-sixteenths of an inch of nail and it was promptly clinched down with the tongs on the nail head and the hammer striking the broken end.

When he had done this he would put down the horse's leg and straighten his back with a grimace of pain as the rheumatics got him. The smith then dragged a three-legged iron stool towards the leg and from the front of the leg he would lift it on to this stool. With his crude home-made hoof cutter (made from an old shoeing rasp: it had to be hammered through the hoof material as this was so hard) he would remove any surplus hoof outside the shoe, and there was never much. He would check the clinches on the ends of the nails and then with a shoeing rasp would rasp the hoof to fit the shoe. This made the nail ends shine and gave a smart finish to the job. It was finished now unless the owner wanted the hoof painted with black Stockholm tar.

A part of the hoof the smith took particular care over was the 'frog' or that triangular rubbery mass in the centre of the hoof. Sometimes he cut bits off with a knife with a turned up end, and then this frog would get a coat of Stockholm tar, which acted as an antiseptic. Sometimes a frog would be torn or bleeding and the hoofs splayed and cracked because they had been left unshod for too long. I have heard the smith say in anger to the man who brought the horse (who was sometimes the owner), 'Thee ought to be shot, this poor bugger's been in agony. If you don't get the vet to un I'll report yer'. Sometimes there were maggots in the hoof.

For a complete set of new shoes the blacksmith at that time charged 10/6d (52^1/2p today).

Both the harness maker at Shipton and our blacksmith were old fashioned Tories determined to be content with their lot. Both read the *Daily Mail* and believed every word that was written; they often told listeners of what they had read as if they owned the only newspapers ever issued. While other men grumbled at their disgustingly low wages and sometimes received an hourly increase of ^{1}/2d or even 1d an hour, these two gentlemen would still be charging the old rates, working hard and skilfully for next to nothing. Even in 1946 when I wanted some gutter irons made for the house I was building, the blacksmith was only charging 4^1/2d each even after he had weighed the iron, at that time costing 3d a lb. For the galvanised strap and its rivet which held it together and his labour, he was charging only 1^1/2d. It was impossible for the man to make any decent living at these prices and any attempt to offer more was curtly refused. A blacksmith at Kingham told me after Mr. Andrews' death that during the war a deputation of local smiths (and there was one in each village) went to see Mr. Andrews to get him to increase his prices in line with theirs. It took a long time talking and a few threats to get 'Jim' Andrews to agree that for the duration he would comply. After the war he went back to his old prices.

For rainy days

For all his Tory sympathies, Old Jim was a well liked figure who in his time was a fair cricketer and umpire. He also ran the Conservative 'Slate Club', as it was called, once a week. On Friday night Jim had his one night out and was quite smart in his old brown suit and trilby hat as he walked to the Swan with his ledgers under his arm and a bag filled with payment cards handed in at his shop rather than at the pub. This was because the payer could not afford to go to the pub as he would be expected to purchase beer while waiting to pay in his weekly subscription. Needless to say this was not very popular with the pub landlord who put a room aside for the Club that night. People paid in 4d per week per person and, after so many payments, if they were sick, they could draw 4/6d for up to six weeks. Needless to say there were people who regularly drew out more in sick pay than they put in. The National Health Service killed off these clubs in 1946–47.

Societies, called Benevolent Societies, flourished in my youth. These met in one or other of the local pubs and indulged in various mysterious activities raising money for their sick members. One of these was the Buffaloes or R.A.O.B. as its full initials were (in full, the Royal and Ancient Order of Buffaloes). I was enthusiastic when I was sponsored to join and wholeheartedly indulged in its activities until I realised that 'Worthy Primos', a sort of N.C.O., and 'Knights', the big noises who were most regular, said most but did least. Money was raised by a system of fines at the meetings when items of everyday consumption were given a different name by the Buffaloes. If a member forgot and called tobacco 'tobacco' instead of 'weed', he would be fined 2d… and so on. I made up my mind that I could buy an insurance policy for myself with what I paid in fines on purpose. One Buffalo who did not believe in insurance, so he told me, was killed the following week, when a tree fell on him. His widow got nothing except a Buffalo funeral for her husband. I left the Buffaloes. These societies and clubs had done a lot of good in their time but had become obsolete.

If a person did not belong to a club or society and fell on bad times, becoming ill, out of work, and thus impoverished, he or she had to 'go on the Parish' which would dole a few loaves, some coal and a few pence with which the poor would have to make do, relying on the goodwill of others or their relatives for relief.

When such a person died, the Parish had to bury them, and a pauper's funeral was something all people dreaded; the plain unvarnished coffin without handles told the whole world, 'Here comes a pauper — a failure'.

'Lloyd George's Pension' or the old age pension had not been in force long when I was born. I believe it started at 5/- a week going up to 10/- by 1947. By that year the Labour Government, elected in 1945, had brought in a vast number of improvements for all, and the workers in particular, including the National Health Service, £30 death grants to help with burying the dead, children's allowances, pit-head baths for the miners who no longer took their dirt home, home help for the sick and aged, and free milk for babies and young school children, to name a few.

The end of the workhouse

The workhouse, that time-honoured repository for the aged, infirm and workless workers, was also scrapped by Labour. Various grants, increased pensions and geriatric wards in hospitals were brought in to help the worker in his or her retirement and made their lot much better than it had been, but even today it is far from perfect.

The end of the tied cottage was another Labour benefit. The 5/- agricultural cottage, as Council Houses were called when first built, were put up to provide the agricultural worker with a house free from his master's right to evict him. It gave him security of housing in his old age. It was not long before various Labour governments, but very few Tory governments, were building thousands of houses through local councils to provide cheap rented housing for the masses.

There had once been a workhouse in our village about forty years before I was born. It was situated among the number of cottages standing on that area between the blacksmith's house and two cottages (now one) facing onto the churchyard, one of which was occupied by 'Chips' Sherborne. These other cottages, now gone, extended on to the end of Chance's house next to Thomas Moss's yard, and the bottom half of one cottage wall can still be seen.

My father said that in his youth, the 1880s and 1890s, it was extremely difficult to carry a coffin up the passage between the cottages to the churchyard. I now have a painting of the forge showing its extension of 1893, and photographs showing 'Workhouse Alley', a path cut through the boundary wall and garden at the end of the blacksmith's house.

Those men who used the workhouse had to pay their way by breaking stones in the village pound, which is a stone-walled enclosure at the bottom end of the churchyard. This pound was also used to impound stray cattle until collected.

George Harry Moss (1886-1961) sitting on a steam roller, about 1910, with roller gang.

White roads

In my younger days the roads were what were called 'white roads'. That is, they were made basically of limestone, broken and levelled and rolled into the road by the broad iron tyres of heavy loaded farm waggons. These iron tyres ground the surface of the limestone into dust which fell into and filled the crevices between the stones and formed a cement when the rains came. Some of this ground stone was washed to the road verges where it was eagerly collected by local builders because it made a very fatty limestone mortar for building purposes.

A man called George Moss was the road contractor responsible for Ascott's roads up to the time the County Council took them over and metalled them as they are today. He once sacked his own son for being one minute late for work. I remember him in his retirement.

I remember as a child in the school yard when the first 'Blue Archells', or egg-sized shaped bits of blue granite, were rolled into the white roads by steam rollers, washed with much water as they rolled. Gangs of men laid the Archells on the scarified surface so that the roller could push them well into the road. After a long length of road had been so 'metalled', the surface was brushed with hot tar dripping from a forty gallon tank fixed over a mobile fire to heat it. The tar ran out of the barrel into large water cans and was then brushed over the road surface by men using stiff brooms. As this gang moved forward another gang and a horse cart filled with gravel followed behind. The gravel was flung with shovels over this tar and there was a certain amount of skill required to throw gravel this way and to cover the tar evenly. It was then rolled in by the steam roller. The men had their trouser bottoms hoisted up by York straps around and below the knee. Their boots were covered with tar which entered the lace holes. It must have been sheer hell to get those boots off at night and on in the morning, and for the woman of the house it must have been the last straw.

However, within a few years the tar was put straight on to the brooms from the tar barrel via pipes connecting broom to barrel. Granite chippings took the place of gravel and these were spread evenly on the tar from a spreader attachment fixed to the back of a cart. Today miles of tar and chippings are put down by small gangs using special machines.

Each village had its 'lengthmen' employed by the County Council. These men formed the bulk of the tarring gangs, but when not doing this they were employed cutting out and keeping clean the 'runnels' cut in the grass verges to run the water off the roads. They also cut the grass on the road verges with scythes and swept and cleaned the kerbs and road edges using a wooden wheelbarrow, a spade and shovel and a large stiff broom. Theirs was a lonely job; yet these men seemed happy enough and did a good job until reorganisation meant that contract gangs with special machines were employed to do their jobs and they became redundant.

Charlie Cook was a foreman in charge of a number of these lengthmen and had to pass many pubs on his cycle while on his tour of inspection. He sometimes stopped at these pubs which were open all day. One day his inspector, out to check on the foreman and his men, came across a cycle half on the road and half in the ditch. In the ditch was Charlie Cook, drunk as a lord. He was sacked on the spot. I remember him coming home and slamming his bike against the wall of his house and cursing as he went indoors to his wife. For the next few months Charlie did small jobs to earn his crust.

'They baint no good yew, ain't got no yuds'

One result of my association with the blacksmith came when I was sweeping out the stable after a number of shoeings. I suddenly thought that I could use those broken three-quarter inch ends of horseshoe nails and so I started to collect them until the blacksmith saw me and asked me what I was doing with them. When I said that I hoped to use them to nail wood together to make rabbit hutches he laughed and said, 'They baint no good yew, ain't got no yuds.' Well, I was to prove him wrong.

Charlie Cook next door now had a donkey and cart. The donkey was called Jenny and lived in the orchard, as we called it, at the back of Slasher Moss's yard. It was surrounded by a hedgerow on one side and Cook's garden wall and sheds on the others. There had been many apple and pear trees there once but now there are few. It is part of 'Waterloo' field now. I have a photo of myself, my brother and sister seated on cushions in front of a dried manure heap, with apple blossom overhead. Charlie and Jenny would go to Milton-under-Wychwood to Alfred Groves, the builders and timber merchants, and get a load of wood blocks for 5/-. The wood was mixed elm, oak and ash and it burnt well. When Charlie had loaded his cart he would go to the nearest pub, the Quart Pot, and drink his fill. The donkey and cart would be in the pub yard waiting for him. If Charlie failed to come out of the pub when Jenny thought he should, she would trot off home on her own and there she would be found when Charlie was brought back by one of his cronies.

At this time a self-employed man named Puffet worked in Groves Yard making boxes out of thin elm wood for tin plate. His thumbs and forefinger were like spoons where he had hit them often with his hammer as he nailed the boards to the ends with one blow per nail. The boards he rejected because of rotten knots, bits broken off or wrong size, were used by Charlie Cook to raise the sides of his cart and thus hold more blocks. Some of those boards stacked around the blocks came my way, and with those three-quarter inch bits of horseshoe nail I managed to make some rabbit hutches; they were very serviceable so long as the wood was damp, but sun and wind caused elm to shrink and twist and become useless.

Charlie Cook liked his beer and was always able to consume more than he could buy with the 6d doled out to him each night by his wife Ada. His size, loud voice and aggressive attitude caused those he rubbed against to buy him beer to get on his good side and ingratiate themselves with him. Life became easier for them that way.

Village life and the Tiddy Hall

Whether electricity or the phone came first I can't remember, except that there was not much time between, and that both of them made a great impact on village life.

Before the arrival of the phone, urgent local messages were sent by bicycle, or further afield by telegraph from Shipton-under-Wychwood post office. Occasionally the man in the signal box would telegraph a message along the line and somehow urgent messages got through that way. Other than the above means there was our post office which at that early stage in my life was

Flo and Doris White outside the Tiddy Hall, probably in the 1920s.

in the first house on the left going up London Lane, owned by Mr. Charlie White, the village cobbler who also made boots. Mrs. White had been a Moss before her marriage and her daughters were rising lights in the village social affairs, especially if they involved the Tiddy Hall and Country Dancing. One of them, Doris, ran the post office while her sister Florence (Flo) became a school teacher. It is still possible to see where the post box was built into their house wall. [*My Personal Memories* by Doris Warner (née White) form the second part of this book.]

Mr. White collected butterflies, and often I would take a capture to him hoping to have caught something rare and thus collect his sixpence. Too often he would say, 'Oh! That's only a Common White,' or other disappointing catch.

His daughters were great cyclists and went miles on their machines usually wearing a fresh hat made from a redesigned and retrimmed old one. They were noted for their hats and cycles, and for their participation in village activities. These took place either in the open air of the Vicarage Garden, or at the 'Tiddy Hall'. This hall, made of wood with a sprung dancing floor and metal roof, was erected by a Mr. Tiddy, a benefactor of the village, in 1912. His son, Lt. Tiddy, was killed during the First World War, and a plaque to his memory is placed inside the Hall. This hall took the place of the old 'Reading Room', an old cottage fitted up as a library which, after World War II, became Dr. Scott's surgery, alas now gone.

The Tiddy Hall was well patronised by village dances, plays, W.E.A. lectures, lantern slides, and Dr. Croly's concerts. This Charlbury doctor and his friends, Dr. Cheadle from Burford and Nurse Roan, gave a concert every year. Here the valiant doctors sang songs without the help of microphones and backing bands, but to the strains of an ancient piano. We heard and enjoyed sketches such as 'The Eye of the Little Yellow God', and heard such poems as 'Vitae Lampada' and the 'Torch of Life' spoken by the schoolmaster or one of the many volunteers, who sang songs which are long since gone, such as Jim Faulkener's 'Needle Cases' which became a hardy annual.

Jim Faulkener was a shepherd who had a nationally known brother, Shepherd Faulkener from Shipton. Jim was not so well known. He was a short thick set man with a rolling gait, usually dressed in breeches and gaiters and he carried a stick. Jim loved to play dominoes at the Swan, but hated to lose. His enemy and friend in these games was the landlord, Mr. Gardner, a retired railway inspector. Mr. Gardner had a bad foot and walked with a limp; he also had – as far as I can remember – the last wax pointed moustache worn by an Ascott man. He had had several wives and fourteen children. Two boys of his were killed in the First World War, yet in the second war his final child was still at school. He was as strong as a horse for all his age and disability, and I and my friends had many a happy time listening to Mr. Gardner and Jim Faulkener cursing each other for cheating as they played dominoes or crib.

Bonfire night

The green, now reasonably tidy and kept well shorn and free from vehicles, has been another and much older centre of village life. Until the mid sixties the annual bonfire was lit on November 5th, the material for the fire being brought in later years by householders in their cars or farmers in their pick-ups. Builders donated old doors etc. and young lads went the rounds collecting from villagers to make their fire as good as, or better than, the one in the next village. However, the resultant mess of unburnt paper, wire from tyres, unburnt wood and the dirty, smelly ashes, were always left for the elements to disperse, the larger unburnt materials being removed unwillingly by people to whom the mess was an affront. So fires on the green were banned. A farmer, H. Cook, allowed the youngsters to have their fire near the river in one of his fields but had to put a stop to this practice because he had to do the clearing up.

When the fire on the green burnt down to its final ashes, people leaving the Churchill Arms as it closed for the night would drag the metal 'Jubilee' seat close to it from across road. On this seat the revellers would sit and drink and eat roast potatoes. Sometimes a departing friend would turn round suddenly and toss a railway detonator into the ashes. The seat and its occupants would fall back and there would be a mad move to escape before the detonator exploded. It was a stupid thing to do, but youth at all times will indulge in dangerous pranks first and think afterwards. Every year that black patch would regenerate itself and boys and girls would play games from out of their school or football at night. Even baseball was played there until broken windows and spokes in the wheels of cycles broken by a speeding ball put a stop to that. The whole business of games on the green was resolved by the opening of a playing field up the High Street after World War II.

Foxhounds used to meet twice a year on the green and, although I am against this obscene sport, I have to admit that the hunt with its many coloured clothes and dogs was a stirring sight. For some reason not made public the Heythrop Hunt suddenly stopped meeting at Ascott. I think one or two of the more advanced farmers disliked gates being left open, and disturbance of stock, as more and more followers used cars to follow the hunt.

Church outings and camp meetings

In the twenties and thirties 'Camp Meetings' or mobile religious meetings were held on the green. A hay waggon was put on the green as a pulpit and people of all denominations leant against the school and other walls or sat on the few chairs, to take part in, or just listen to, the services which were held mainly by the Baptist Churches. More people attended these meetings than went to Church or Chapel, and people from other villages attended. In my time a Mr. Viner from Witney was the main speaker and was a well known Witney business man.

As children up to the age of fourteen, when we should normally leave school, we were expected to go to Church three times on Sundays and join the choir if invited. There were also Bible classes in the afternoon. Being in the choir had its compensations, the white surplice covered our everyday clothes as we had no Sunday best as such, and of course for a few years there was a 'choir outing' to Stratford-on-Avon, where we were given a tea of cakes and sandwiches and taken for boat rides on the Avon. The coach ride there and back was as much a treat as the events in Stratford. Some clever lads somehow contrived to get to both Church and Chapel outings. I well remember the wrath of our vicar when he found out about this.

Church and Chapel did not mix at the top; indeed the Pastor of the Chapel and the Vicar of the Church would cross the road rather than pass on the same pavement. It is a good job that such bigotry appears to have gone, and sad that the influence of the Pastor and Vicar on the village people has declined steadily since the end of the last War.

The old-fashioned Christmas

Our Christmases as children were in some respects much better than we have today; they were more cosy family affairs centred about the hearth. As far as material benefits go, today's Christmas gifts, with the vast range to choose from, can be regarded as far better than those of years gone by. But I wonder? I am sure more happiness and thanks were given by the toys of yester year than by the sophisticated toys of today, more so since yesterday's toys were given on specified days while today's toys are bought at any time. The lovely air of expectancy and excitement are gone. I doubt if as many children go to bed early to await the coming of Father Christmas now as did when I was young. Of course we suffered disappointments with our toys when the family purse was empty, and often we had to be satisfied with an apple, an orange, some nuts and a bit of coal in our socks instead of that shiny tin popgun from Woolworths costing a precious 6d.

Also there was more aftermath to the Christmases of yesteryear which lingered on until New Year's Day had passed.

If we as children were disappointed with our toys, we were seldom disappointed with our food as we usually had a 'barnyard rooster' for dinner and a large Christmas pudding. The roosters were far superior to any polythene-clad chicken of today, but of course today everyone has a turkey for Christmas, since they have become so commonplace and cheap. The pudding would contain silver 3d pieces or sixpences. Most years these had to be handed back as money was very tight and we were getting into the hard harsh days of the recession when 3,000,000 breadwinners became out of work. Sometimes we had an iced cake costing 4/6d to go with Mum's mincepies, and perhaps a packet of 6d crackers.

After tea, and when the pubs opened one hour later as on a Sunday, my elder brothers would go there to collect the free pint the landlord sometimes gave on Christmas day. This left Mum and Dad and four or five children who would help mother clear away, and then wash up for her, so that she could have a few minutes 'peace' at the fire. Dad would be in his usual chair smoking his pipe, which was seldom out of his mouth, and either reading yesterday's newspaper again or the jokes we had found in our crackers. Sometimes these 6d-a-dozen crackers would contain one of those tin frogs which, when squeezed, gave off a hard snapping sound. Our parents would put up with the noise for a while and then forbid us to use it again that night.

Often the toys so eagerly unwrapped in the early hours of the morning would be broken or bent by bedtime on Christmas Day. Those cheap clock-work engines would lose their wheels so shoddily put on, or the cheap spring of the motor would have twanged for the last time. Many times Christmas Day ended in tears as frustrated children, who had had a long day, went off to bed, to listen to parents talking below until drowsiness turned into full sleep. On Boxing Day, after futile attempts to repair the engine, the little clips holding the pieces together would have been broken off and the body of the train 'Made in Germany' would be revealed as having been a Tate & Lyle Golden Syrup tin in a previous life. The name of the firm and the dead lion badge were all too obvious.

Somehow there was always snow over Christmastide, and carol singers with their lanthorns of guttering candles in glass cages would be welcome as they sang their offerings before knocking at the door. When I became old enough to join the Church choir, I went around the village for three nights before Christmas and very often ended up with a sore throat and chest as the vicious cold of those frosty nights went right through me.

Before school started again there would be two weeks of snow fights and sliding on the icy roads, much to the annoyance of older people who slipped on the slides we had made. Sometimes crude sledges appeared made from planks of wood or old sheets of metal, there being many hills around for sledging. The rivers flooded often in winter and frosts always seemed severe enough to freeze the floods hard enough for children and some adults to slide on long into the evenings. As winter eased into spring, wooden tops bought for ½d and called window breakers appeared on the dusty wind-swept roads, whipped along by the stick and string whips of the children. These tops sped fast and, as their name implies, were responsible for many broken windows. Fatter, slower tops called turnip tops were used more by girls who could whip the larger bulk of this top better than the slim window breaker. All these tops were a nuisance to cyclists and pedestrians alike and, like the iron hoops, gradually faded from the schoolchild's playthings as the increasing number of cars made their use on the roads a nightmare.

Marbles had been a playground game enjoyed by noisy quarrelsome youngsters, mostly boys, but had disappeared from use by the mid thirties. The girls enjoyed their skipping and hopscotch, even on that horrible rough playground, now covered by tarmac and grass. Cricket, football and leapfrog were played on the green, and also cruel and crude games were played on some newcomers if they appeared to be cocky or too independent.

A very unofficial game

The older boys who left school at 14 were not all angels, and clever newcomers were soon put in their place. There was a very unofficial game called 'Jack up the drainpipe' where the one to be taken down a peg or two was persuaded that no-one could beat the drainpipe crawling record of the time. The drainpipe was made by a line of boys standing with their legs apart to form the drain. On the word *Go*, the challenger got down on hands and knees and started to crawl through these lines of legs. As soon as he was inside the ends of the drain were closed, and the boys in the middle of the drain urinated on the one crawling through. It did not pay the boy victim to complain about his treatment; if he did he was seldom without black eyes to compensate for the weals on the backsides of his tormentors.

With the spring's longer evenings, as in the autumn, village boys would play a game called 'fox and hounds'. A volunteer would act as the fox and would disappear into the gloom. He was given two or three hundred yards start and then he would be chased by the pack who would shout to him 'Holler! Holler! Holler! and the dogs will follow'. The fox would 'holler' or 'hello!' once or twice and about every five minutes, leading the pack through muddy yards and places where cattle had churned up the mud by gateways, until he got back to the starting point or was caught on the way. No great harm was done; sometimes an irate farmer would bellow threats if the stock in his yard was disturbed. It was our parents who grumbled most as we came home with wet, dirty clothes and boots. In our early days we kept away from farms where fathers worked, as it sometimes went badly for the parent if his son got up to trouble on the ground where his father was employed.

By the same token I was always sure of a hiding if any other lads had been seen on 'Coopers' Railway Bridge, and had been throwing stones at the trains. Railwaymen were jealous of their jobs, considered to be one up on the farm labourer, and paid about five shillings a week more. They would certainly lose their jobs if one of their children were caught throwing stones at passing engines, and so we automatically got a belting to 'larn' us to keep away from the trains. Unfair? Well, maybe, but very understandable; throwing stones at trains was a stupid thing to do and very dangerous, and it could have caused a terrible accident.

I bore no grudge for those hidings: yet I would never forget a jibe against our poverty and, as I grew into manhood, certainly gave back with interest those insults I had to take as a child. When the Second World War came and five of Dad's sons went to war, I certainly reminded those whose children I had grown up with, but who got 'reserved' jobs at home, of the sneers they had made some ten years or more earlier.

Lavatory humour

Not only did young teenagers get into scrapes, older teenagers and young men in their early twenties relieved the sameness of their daily existence with stupid, but to them hilarious, pranks. One young man, named Jack Honeybone, who liked his beer but was not noted for his intelligence, was usually among the ring leaders when trouble was about.

The old sexton's name was Edginton, nicknamed 'Pecker' because of the short-handled pick he carried when walking to the churchyard to dig a grave. Old Jim, as I called him, because I used to help him fill in graves or work around the churchyard weeding etc., sometimes gave me a copper or two and so I tagged along whenever I could. Old Jim did other jobs at night to increase his income, and one of these was cleaning out the school toilet vaults. With another elderly man he would hire a horse and cart and take it into the school yard and put a deep layer of ashes on the bottom of the cart. With the cart drawn up near the porch the two old men started their unpleasant job with ladles and buckets, emptying the contents on top of the ashes in the cart. To fill their buckets took several minutes, plenty of time for Honeybone to nip over the school wall and undo the girth straps and chains which held the shafts of the cart to the horse. As the patient old horse stood still and the weight of the shafts pushed down on the harness, the cart appeared to be normal until suddenly the weight of the contents of the last two buckets altered the centre of gravity of the cart. Up went the shafts, down went the back of the cart, and out shot its contents over the luckless labourers in charge. The culprit in the darkness beyond the range of the lantern lights saw the results of his handiwork and, grinning, went off to the pub to tell his cronies. Poor old Jim and his companion, Mr. Jimmy Wilkins, had that mess to clear up. They got the sympathy of the village and that was all.

The yob concerned got away with it, to repeat it in a different way a few weeks later outside the village schoolhouse. Whether he had it in for Old Jim or whether he took any chance he got to get up to mischief, I don't know, but one dark night about a month later as he was going through the churchyard to the Swan, he noticed lantern lights to his left by the schoolhouse. He walked past gravestones towards these lights, and saw Old Jim and Jimmy Wilkins emptying the schoolhouse vaults into a ring of ashes under the high churchyard wall. This stone wall had loose topping stones laid flat, about 24 inches x 18 inches each. Honeybone got to his knees and crept towards where the action was. As he saw the lights of the lanterns approaching him he lay flat on his stomach, his hands gripping the stone in line with the hole in the ring of ashes. When he heard the 'plop' of the buckets being emptied he gave that stone a strong push and it fell into the noisome mess below, splashing the two Jims all over.

Now Old Jim was never known to swear, other than 'Well, I'm pothered', but that night he said words best not repeated. (Incidentally Old Jim always described bottles as pottles, a mode of definition sixty years or more out of date.)

Honeybone's Ascott family was a little older than mine, both going back to the Civil War, but his family has now gone from the village and the last male died in the eighties.

More pranks

'Window tapping' was a prank practised by younger teenagers who would fasten a button a few inches from one end of a length of cotton. This end would have been pinned to the window frame of a victim's cottage. This would, of course, be at night, and when the pranksters and the other end of the cotton were in a place of concealment, the cotton would be shaken to make the button tap against the window glass. After a while the curtains would be opened and a face would be seen pressed against the glass. After a few moments the curtains would be shut and the 'Tap! Tap! Tap!' of the button would start again. After a bit the window would be opened and a head would appear to look up and down the road. Mystified, the head would disappear and the tapping would recommence.

Now the irate cottager would run round to the front of his house while someone within would open the curtains and let the light shine out. A quick look round would find the cotton and button, and a red-faced man would look in the direction indicated by the cotton and raise his fist to the sky. 'You dang young varmints! I knows yer! Wait till I tells yer dad, he'ull larrop yer.' He would snatch the cotton and button and disappear indoors. Once settled indoors he would probably hear a handful of grit being thrown against his window as a final provocation, and the pranksters would move elsewhere. The cottages in the Row facing the churchyard, with its gigantic guardians of chestnut trees, were the favourite target as the churchyard gave the safest concealment.

Another prank concerning the cottages in the Row happened in my pre-teen years. This row of cottages was built for a charity for £18 the shell. The shell was then divided by chimney-breasts of stone to make seven cottages which then had lath and plaster sub divisions. Labourers lived in these cottages, most of them amicably; some, however, could live with no-one for long without falling out with them.

At the bottom end of this row lived two families who could not stand the sight of each other. Their doors were always ajar in the daytime so that they could hear any conversations which occurred with the people next door. A youth called Keep and his cronies decided one day to stir up these two families, so Keep went into the first garden nearest the road and cut the rope clothes line. With this rope they carefully made slip-knot nooses which they put over the two door knockers. Having tied the ropes so that they could not be slipped open, Keep then hammered on the door of 'Cocky' Edginton. When Edginton tried to open his door he pulled his neighbour's door shut with a bang. This banging of his door brought Edginton's neighbour, Prissie Edginton, to his door which he tried to open and so pulled shut Cocky Edginton's door. There they were, two men who hated each other, slam-banging each other's doors and uttering bloodthirsty threats of what they would do 'when I gits outa yer'. A passer-by cut them loose and all was revealed, and the police were called. Because the culprit could not be found, a constable came to the school and stood in front of the senior class. 'Since no-one will own up you will all have to bring ½d to school tomorrow to pay for that line, or you will all go to court'. It worked, all boys in that class brought ½d and in time the event was forgotten. I just wonder what that constable would have done if some parent had said, 'I'm not paying, find the culprit and make him pay the lot'.

For the line cutting, needless to say, many boys had sore backsides when their fathers heard of it.

Cocky Edginton married my father's sister and was my uncle. Like all the Edgintons he was a big man, and very strong as they all had to be in those days. Wheat was bagged in 2¼ cwt sacks called a 'quarten'. Cocky could lift one in his teeth while ordinary men could not move one by hands and arms.

Half-holidays and old festivities

Maundy Thursday and Ascension Day were two half-day holidays for our school, and we loved them. Maundy Thursday was the day H. M. The King gave out the Maundy Money. On both days we assembled at school as usual and then about 10 o'clock made our way to Church.

Somehow those two days were always sunlit and warm. As we walked up the path to the church we saw clouds of butterflies fluttering in the church-yard. After church on those two days we had our holiday in the afternoon. It might be spent bird nesting or in sport on the green; more likely it led to a session on either of Dad's two allotments.

The sound of grasshoppers in the turf and the sight of many wild flowers growing in the long grass on the unused portion of the graveyard, are memories of an England which died with World War II. The coming of intensive farming included the use of herbicides and insecticides, which killed off wild flowers and insects wherever applied. We still hear and see doves in the trees but they are not the 'Blue Rock Doves' of yesteryear, but a beige coloured bird imported about thirty years ago, and which has now become so widespread that it is now classed as a pest.

Only once since 1946 have I seen a cloud of butterflies which in number anywhere nearly approached the clouds of pre-war times, and that was in that glorious very hot year of 1976. Wood pigeons which were counted in thousands per flock now have a job to raise fifty at a time in this area.

On Palm Sundays, for some reason never really explained to me, Mother bought liquorice root and knobs of black liquorice were smashed up and put in corked bottles filled with water. These bottles were then well shaken to produce a brown liquid which was eagerly drunk by small mouths. Of course we were sent to church where the Vicar gave out reeds representing the palms put before Christ on his entry into Jerusalem.

Relics of the old Victorian attitudes still remained in certain quarters. The churchwardens were farmers and also school managers, who would without hesitation ask labouring persons why they were not in church last Sunday. The truants would be reminded that this was an offence at law and there was still on the statute book powers to enable the offender to be fined 40/- for his absence. These farmers always sat in the same pews and no-one else was allowed to use them. The farmers would keep their eyes on us and would often tell off a choirboy for not attending to his duties during the service.

The maypole was very much in use when I was a child and no social event in the open air took place without its maypole dancing. The dancers always got applause, especially if it was a good display, and I still think that this and morris dancing should be kept up and seen more often. The maypole was in use at Ascott School up to 1987/88 when the school closed because of a drop in pupil numbers. Thank heaven it was saved by outsiders from Burford who now run the school for Burford and district children as a private venture. Sadly for me, the house I built next door has been used for classrooms and my garden as a playground.

Besides the maypole which was used on other occasions than May 1st (or Labour Day as it is sometimes called), there was a custom in my youth which was devoted to that one day. Primroses and cowslips were abundant in my youth, and violets bloomed in the hedgerows of London Lane. With great masses of cowslips tied around a stick looking like a huge candyfloss of flowers, I and my younger brothers and sister were urged to go from door to door with this garland and sing:

> Maypole, Maypole, trot, trot, trot,
> See what a Maypole we have got,
> Garlands high, garlands low,
> Maypole, Maypole, trot, trot, trot.

I remember we once collected the enormous sum of 4/6d in pennies and halfpennies. This custom stopped when Fred Alden made a complaint to the police saying it was begging. Perhaps it was, but as Mother said, it had gone on all the time she had lived and no-one was compelled to give anything. As far as I can remember Alden was the only person who ever complained but then others of his ilk put an end to carol singing by children at Christmas. Now they are supposed to sing for a charity and have to get police permission beforehand. It is a pity we could not retaliate and put an end to the fox hunting and horse betting which Alden, now dead, had loved so much; for much money which could have been better used in feeding and clothing children went into bookmakers' pockets.

Planting the potatoes ...

Summer time meant days on the allotments watering plants, hoeing, weeding, digging, planting and a never-ending series of essential jobs. It was also a convivial time as the allotments comprised fifty acres of ground divided into quarter-acre plots of which perhaps eight acres were taken by four persons and the remaining 168 plots by solo tenants. The clack of a myriad forks on brashy ground, the cries of children, the barking of dogs and, if no women or children were close, the jokes of the men shouted across from piece to piece, gave much to talk over when the men had gone home to their wives.

Water had to be carried from a stand pipe below the vicarage, and this was a job often given us by Father when we came out of school. Often we slopped as much as half of the water by the time we reached the cabbage patch, and Dad expected to see a large wet patch around each one when he came up later on. We used an old soup tin for this and doled out the water to make it go as far as we could. When a cabbage was cut we had to make a large cross on the old stem top, and in due course we got four cabbage sprouts from this. Vacant ground had to be dug and kept clean, then spread with pig muck to be dug in later.

On Good Friday, the first holiday of the year for my father, the new unofficial allotment year started, as it was hoped to get the first early potatoes planted then. This planting occupied the gardener for many evenings, and Saturdays, as potatoes formed the largest and most valuable crop to be planted. There was an everlasting search for fresh seed potatoes without the cost of buying Scotch seed. Sometimes swaps were made with friends in the next village or farther afield in the hope of finding a variety which would increase our yield. Often the 'seed' potatoes had to be small bantam egg-sized potatoes of our own, saved from last year's crop. It was hoped to use fresh ground for the potatoes each year in order to give some kind of rotation of crops. Small hands would take the potatoes out of their hessian sacks and fill buckets with them trying not to break off any of the 'chits' or new growth.

The next eldest would have the job of placing the potatoes in the furrow dug out for them by their elders. A stick, the right length for the particular type of potato, would be used to place the potatoes the correct distance apart. These potatoes had to be pushed into the dug earth lightly, about four inches up from the bottom of the furrow with the 'eyes' or 'chits' uppermost. After a few hours using the stick, this would be discarded and we had to judge the distance by eye.

The planting line, wound each end around two strong pointed sticks, would be moved back eighteen to twenty inches according to Dad's orders, and then those with forks would cover over the potatoes and dig back to the line to form a furrow for the next row. So the work proceeded, and soon young backs would begin to ache. As soon as Dad thought you were old enough to use a fork you were given one. In a way it was a sign that you counted as a man now as far as work went, because if you could use a fork you could use a hoe or a spade, and what else did one want in order to cultivate the soil?

Having planted our potatoes, we then had weeks of work looking after them. Moulding up the soil around the plants as soon as they were a few inches above ground was only the first of many operations of care of the crops. As their growth increased, more moulding up was done to the potatoes, but this double moulding usually applied to the early potatoes only. Because of the other planting taking place about this time, of broad beans, peas, and various vegetables such as carrots, parsnips, onions, etc., the later variety of potatoes was well through the ground by the time moulding up could be done and so this operation was completed at one go. During the growing season there was plenty of hoeing to be done between the various crops, and the hand weeding of those potatoes that had been moulded up.

At harvest time the potatoes were dug up, allowed a few hours to dry in the sun and then picked up. During this process the soil, or as much as was possible, was rubbed from the tubers and all damaged, green or small potatoes removed to be used as pig food, except for the ones gone bad. If the crop was a good one and there were more potatoes than could be stored at home, the surplus was put into 'clamps' for winter storage. In clamps the potatoes are stacked on a straw bed, covered with straw and then with about nine inches of soil all over, with the surface tamped tight and smooth with the back of a spade. There would be a small trench at the outside of the clamp for drainage. These clamps remained untouched until the potatoes were required, then all of them would be taken home and put in our 'hovel' or store shed, care being taken that no chitted or bad potatoes were allowed in. At the end of the season, and before the new potatoes of the new year arrived, the children of the family usually had the disliked job of 'chitting' the potatoes, which meant rubbing off any young sprouting chits from the tubers, a long distasteful job as stored potatoes sweated and were messy.

The best tasting potatoes came from the cottage back garden where the soil was black, rich and up to two feet thick due to the thousands of buckets of night soil buried there over the years. This objectionable but necessary operation was carried out in the dark when a hole two feet deep and eighteen inches square would be dug. The night soil bucket would be removed from under the seat in that little stone built shed 'down the garden', and its contents would be emptied into the hole. The bucket had to be swabbed out and cleaned with the head of an old 'soft' broom. A little Jeyes Fluid would be put in the bucket to 'sweeten' it and it would be replaced. This job had to be done at least four times a week. A bucket lasted about three years before the landlord provided a new one. We planted runner beans and also a few broad beans in this garden, so that if Mother was short of stuff from the allotment she could make up from her garden. Parsnips were a favourite crop and grew well in that deep soil, to be used for wine making as well as cooking.

Of course our neighbours, the Cooks, were one up on us in this as in most things. Their 'closet down the garden' had a seat for three people with the middle small one for a child. They had no buckets but a vault under the seat which was emptied by Mr. James Edginton and Jimmy Wilkins once a year. Very often payment for this was a sack of small potatoes each or a chunk of pig's meat, as money was as tight in the Cook family as it was in ours, with the difference that Ada made sure a little something was put by each week out of Charlie's wage.

Cook kept more pigs than we did, simply because he had more room than us, and by using his size and bluster somehow managed to buy them cheaper than we did. With a bosom friend who worked in Cooper's Mill he was never short of barley meal, which was a prime mover when it came to pig rearing.

... and cutting the corn

Sometimes my dad would plant barley on one of his quarter acre plots, hand digging the ground and broadcasting the barley seed by hand, then raking the ground all over. Cook could always find a friend with the right machine to plough up his ground and drill the corn for the price of a few pints.

In due course Dad's barley would be cut with a scythe or a sickle and the eldest children would have to make 'bonds' with the barley or oddments of string, and tie the crop up into bundles. When dry they would be stored under some old sheets of corrugated iron awaiting threshing.

In those days corn was cut with a 'binder', a machine which cut the corn and bound it in regular sized sheaves with the ears all at one end. This machine threw out the sheaves after tying and farm hands would seize them one in each hand and stand them, butts to the ground about a foot apart with the heads leaning towards each other. Six or eight of these sheaves, so placed at about every ten yards, would be called a 'stook' and it was reckoned to allow the stooks to stand for up to three weeks out in the field to dry out all the green weeds and rubbish that had grown at the base of the corn. Sometimes on a sunny, airy day the farmer would order his men out in the field to open the stooks, that is throw them apart for the warmth and air to kill

Busby's rickyard, later Cook's yard, before being re-developed for bungalows.

the damp greenstuff if there was a lot in that crop. If the corn was 'carried', that is collected, and put into ricks before it was properly 'fit', it stood a good chance of overheating and catching fire by spontaneous combustion.

Dad's three or four hundredweight of barley would be taken to one of the two mills at Ascott and ground into meal for the pigs.

Dad's corn would be threshed for him by arrangement with Mr. Joshua Busby, the farmer who owned the farm on the corner of High Street and London Lane opposite to where my children were born. When Mr. Busby hired the steam threshing tackle to thresh his corn, Dad and some other men like him would have their corn ready in heaps and a few sacks ready to use as soon as Mr. Busby had finished.

The bird trap

Peas were a favourite crop of old Mr Busby's. If the pea crop was not heavy, it would be threshed the old-fashioned way with flails. A flail comprised two strong sticks, one shorter than the other, joined with a leather hinge, and was used to beat the pea straw and free the peas, which would then be shaken from the straw and gathered to be used for animal feed and seed.

In the winter we boys used to spread a little pea straw and chaff in the middle of the yard, and prop a large sieve up on a stick about nine inches long, to the middle of which we tied a piece of string long enough to reach the barn doors, which would be almost closed, but not quite. From within we would watch the birds scratching about in the straw and chaff until they got to the few grains of wheat under the sieve. As soon as the birds got to the wheat, the line was pulled, the prop came out and the sieve fell and trapped the birds, which were then disposed of and the trap reset.

Blackbirds, if enough were caught, went into a pie. Sparrows were killed for ferret food. Bullfinches, goldfinches and linnets would be taken home by a man called Harry Chandler who lived in the house next to the entrance to Cook's Yard: he caged them and sold them as pets. Robins and thrushes were set free.

A gleaning story

Sometimes as children we would get a farmer's permission to go 'gleaning' after the corn had been carried. Four or five youngsters urged on by the thought that they were helping Mum would soon pick up a fair amount of ears of corn still on the straw or ears that had broken off.

One year the farmer came to inspect what we had picked up. He was surprised by the amount and wanted half of it, saying we must have been picking the standing corn. Of course we had not done so; even a blind man would know that because what we had picked up was wheat and what was standing was barley.

The same farmer is still remembered today as the man who had knocked the baskets of blackberries out of the hands of two spinster women and trodden the berries into the ground. These 'spinster' daughters of 'Prissey' Edginton were innocent, hard working women, 'a little slow in the yed' as the saying then went. They were well liked and, in spite of their impediments, lived to their late eighties. Such was the authority of the farmers, backed by magistrates, that incidents like this, although long remembered, went unchallenged except when the beer flowed freely in the pub. Since the farmers drank sixpenny tots of whisky in their own little room in the pub, and not in earshot of the public bar, I doubt if they were at all troubled by the beer talk.

Those days the farmers were little better off than their labourers and it would be hard to distinguish between them by the clothes they wore. Both would have holes in their clothes which would be held together, like the field gates, with liberal amounts of binder string.

Village fetes

Fetes were held twice a year at the vicarage. They were held also on occasion at Chestnut Close, a large house built by a shipping magnate called Furness, which lies on the Shipton side of Coldwell Brook and is therefore in Shipton parish. The Furness family did much for the village of Ascott in the way of charity gifts to the poor.

A Mr. Stan Webb who first came to Ascott in 1904 at the age of four has told me of the 'children's treats' which were held at the Tiddy Hall when it was first opened. There were other 'treats' for children given by the church in co-operation with the village folk, when the children were sat at tables and given a few cakes, sandwiches and lemonade. Afterwards, games were played and songs were sung until both children and parent helpers were glad to call it a day. Both parties being content with what they had enjoyed during those few afternoon hours, sometimes these treats were ended by dances for the parents and older children after the youngsters had been taken home.

When the treats were given by the so-called gentry of the village, i.e. the people of Chestnut Close, The Grange and the house next door owned by the Gomes, the event was well publicised and was expected by the givers to be well patronised by village children. When the children arrived at the Tiddy Hall, they we seated at a long table made up of small tables put end to end with chairs on either side. The vicar at another table, flanked by representatives from the gentry, wished the children a happy afternoon with a firm

A fete in Ascott in July 1923 (note the summer clothing!)

reminder of the generosity of the givers and the bounty they were about to receive. The children showed their appreciation by clapping their hands.

After Christmas, this 'bounty' constituted the left-overs of the Christmas parties held by the gentry. It was a cold collection of bits and pieces of pies, cakes and meats not touched by the party goers, and now generously given to the poor and needy of the village children. What there was showed good quality, but was unmistakably left-overs. Of course the children enjoyed the meal as it contained a lot of unaccustomed items of food, but the parent helpers saw and knew the truth. Usually presents were given of unwanted toys and clothes, and I believe the fur-trimmed coat I wore for my debut at school came from such a source.

The vicarage fetes were held on the lawns at the back of the vicarage, and entrance was via the verandah door, after paying the penny or twopence entrance fee at the vicarage gates. The verandah fronted the large pine tree standing at the top of the drive. Sometimes a stall or two would be placed under this verandah, but more often the stalls were placed in a row along the lovely warm red brickwork of the kitchen garden which formed one boundary to the lawns. The fete was usually opened by the vicar at 2.30 p.m. although sometimes a local worthy was available for this function.

The stalls sold the usual articles, such as jams, cakes, fruit, potted plants and bric-a-brac; anything in fact which would bring in a copper or two. There would be plenty of raffles, and cups of tea and lemonade were always available. This lemonade was made in huge jugs from lemonade powder and water.

There were competitions such as the best designed hat for the women, and 'the most beautiful baby' for the matrons among them. This latter usually ended with some bad feeling and accusation of favouritism if a child of a better-off couple won the competition. 'Find the sixpence' was another hoary old game, when people paid 2d and were given a plant label on which they put their name and stuck it in the bit of ground where they hoped the sixpence might be hidden.

A brass band would be in attendance and was often the Salvation Army band or the Chipping Norton Silver Band. It would be seated on that raised dais of soil and turf constructed for the purpose when the lawns were laid out.

Besides the obvious stalls and events mentioned, there would be coconut shies when one paid 2d for three wooden balls in the hope of knocking a coconut off its stand. Donkey rides were also provided and sometimes an awkward animal would enliven the proceedings by refusing to move until goaded by pokes and slaps on the rump. 'Bowling for the pig' was a must for the men who paid 6d for three balls to bowl at the skittles placed on what was not always the most level piece of ground. On occasion, if more than one donkey was available, donkey races would be held and amateur bookmakers were soon in evidence.

At most fetes and village entertainments morris dancers from the village teams performed their dances which had been revived by a Mr. Cecil Sharpe who had sets of leg bells and regalia reproduced by a Mr. William Kimber from a set owned by Mr. Charles White, our village shoemaker. For morris dancing the girls wore white spotted muslin, Dutch bonnets and fichus. Their hair was in two long plaits tied with ribbons, which matched others tied to their shoes. These ribbons were made to match the dresses; the dresses of adult women had a tight bodice and full skirt. The men wore white flannel trousers with coloured baldrics and bells around their legs. Children wore coloured floral print dresses and matching sunbonnets for the girls, while the boys wore Holland smocks with wide hats and red scarves.

Mr. Furness, whose family built Chestnut Close and lived there, used to play his fiddle to accompany the morris dances and jigs, although he was blind. He later became Lord Sanderson and between the wars he and the morris dancers went to local houses of importance, such as Bruern Abbey, Cornwell Manor, Shipton Court, Lee Place, Cornbury Park and numerous others, and to Charlbury.

An innovation was tried one year which could have had serious consequences had it been allowed to continue. A tin bath was half filled with water and 2/6d was placed on the bottom. The public were then invited to spend 3d to have a go at picking up the half crown out of the water. I had a go and as soon as my fingers touched the water I received a tremendous electric shock which compelled me to withdraw my hand. Others had a go, and were treated likewise, all complaining that the shock was too severe. This complaint was upheld by a person with a knowledge of electricity and the event was cancelled; just as well, as it could have killed anyone with a weak heart.

'Empire Day', or the 24th May, was well celebrated in the twenties. A fete would be held at the vicarage as described above, with the addition of much patriotic fervour in the singing of jingoistic songs and flag waving. I remember I was presented with a medal on one of these occasions for something I had done at school. The medal was of aluminium and showed the Prince of Wales, later Edward VIII, on one side, and Britannia, flag wrapped, on the reverse. There was a date, in my case I believe it was 1927, cast into the medal which had a red, white and blue ribbon. I had this medal up to a few years back when it was given to one of my grandchildren.

Folk dancing was very popular between the wars and still has a vigorous survival now.

By 8.30 parents had had enough of their wandering children's frequent demands for pennies and, tired and harassed, they collected them and took them home. Often a few clouts were publicly handed out to their offspring who had misbehaved on the well groomed lawns by jumping across the flower beds and sometimes landing amongst the flowers. Sometimes the nearest adult would administer a cuffed ear to the errant child, and certainly mum would add another for 'showing me up in front of everybody'.

Visiting lecturers

I remember attending W.E.A. lectures in the Tiddy Hall between the wars, and I wish they were still available today. Many notable radio personalities gave lectures there, including Mrs. Mary Stocks, the well known radio personality. Mr. Alan Bullock gave wonderful history lectures and went on to become a famous radio and T.V. lecturer, who later rose high in the hierarchy of the B.B.C. Ruskin College sent down lecturers and Dr. Reginald Jaques organised community singing. During World War II Bill Owen, who played Compo in the 'Last of the Summer Wine' series, was billeted at the Tiddy Hall whilst serving with the Pioneer Corps.

The W.E.A., which did wonderful work, was ousted at the end of the war in favour of the Women's Institute.

The vicarage is now redundant as such, and the village has to share its vicar with two other parishes, whilst the vicar lives at Chadlington. For perhaps six years Pam Ayres, the Oxfordshire poetess, lived in this renovated and enlarged vicarage, until the age of her children made her move elsewhere for their schooling.

Village fetes are now held in the Memorial Playing Field, given to the village by Mr. O. V. Watney of the brewing family after World War II. He was the owner of Cornbury Park Estate at the time and owned more than the village. He has since passed on without an heir.

The cricket field: 'knee-high grass, cowpats and cows'

Between the wars our cricket pitch and two teams gave regular entertainment on Saturday afternoons and some weekday evenings. At that time the cricket pitch was in the first field on the right going over the level crossing towards Chipping Norton. The pitch itself was reasonably level and was maintained by the village lads with a push mower and a large ex-horse-drawn flat roller which was pulled and pushed by the older boys and men, while young children sat on top for the ride and to add weight.

The outfield was a different matter with knee-high grass, cowpats and cows. It all made for good fun and some noble big hitting, some balls ending up at Oxford or London when a passing goods train had a ball drop into an open top truck. Balls have been hit over the railway and into the public house gardens, a feat only bettered by two other men, my brother George and 'Bending' Shayler. These two hit balls over the tops of the elm trees which lined the roadside hedgerow of the field the other side of the road leading to Chippy Hill. The distance has not been measured but I think it is safe to say that the cricket pitch would be at least sixty-five yards from the base of these elm trees, which would be almost forty feet high. That is some hit!

A wooden hut near the railway fence served as a storage shed for equipment and as a scorer's desk, with the details being shown by numbered and lettered steel plates hung on the front face of the building.

Teas were had at the Churchill Arms for 1/- and after the match both teams returned for drinks and games of darts and dominoes etc.

The village pub

Pubs pre-war were so different from the surviving few of today. Not only were there more of them, but they were better patronised until the bicycle and the cinema started to coax the patrons away. Pub buildings were not the tarted up buildings they are today. The windows were often the old iron casements, with leaded lights hung on hook and ride hinges to old oak frames, and by reason of age were ill-fitting and draughty.

The heavy wooden doors were not much better and usually opened into rooms which stank of stale beer, tobacco and wood smoke. The floors were most often stone flagstones worn away by countless hobnailed boots into an uneven surface with open joints in places. Seating was usually a bench around the outside wall with a high backed settle between door and fire to keep away the draughts. Sawdust sprinkled on the floor was on its way out when I started going to the pub, and spitoons, though not so commonly used as before, could often be seen and sometimes used. The colour scheme always seemed to be yellow painted plaster walls and ceilings, and brown painted woodwork. Time would show that the 'yellow' paint on the walls and ceiling was actually white paint tainted yellow by tobacco smoke which, if left untouched long enough, would turn the white into a yellow and then brown.

My favourite pub was the Churchill Arms, now a private house. It was built around 1830 when the Churchill family owned the estate, and the previous pub was situated at Corner House Farm, opposite to where my children were born. When that pub was towards its closing days, it was kept by a Moss whose great great grandson late in 1989 wrote to me asking for information about his family. The vaulted brick interior roof of the cellar is still as it was left when the pub closed, and the steps down into this room are still in good condition.

A young man would 'go to pub' quietly at the beginning until he was accepted as one of the 'regulars' and he would be careful to 'mind his p's and q's', especially before his elders. If his speech was too loud or what he was saying was not to the liking of his elders, he would be sure to be put in his place with a 'Shut yer gob, yew don't know nothing, ain't lived long enough yut'. The speaker would be one of the gnarled old men seated in their favourite seats, as strong as an ox still in spite of a stoop and skin as brown and as wrinkled as a walnut. The rebuke having been administered the speaker would purse his lips and spit eight to ten feet into the fire.

Beer mugs would be kept filled by an ever-watchful landlord who, seeing a glass empty or nearing so, would bring over his jug and top it up, going back to his cellar to refill his jug from the wooden casks on cradles placed on the floor. Slow drinkers were not encouraged in those days as most landlords had to have another job during the day while their wives took over the running of the pub. Anyone seated with an empty glass got it filled whether he wanted it or not, so everyone soon got the message: 'Drink or leave'. No-one stood up but all sat at small tables with a chair on either side or on the benches and settles with a trestle table in front of them.

In thundery weather, beer in the casks would 'go off', change colour and flocculate like sour milk poured into tea. This is where a good landlord or cellarman came into his own, as with hessian sacks soaked with water wrapped around their precious beer barrels, they strove to keep their stock cool and drinkable.

Mild beer cost 4d and bitter 6d 'from the wood' (the cask). Bottled beers were then about 9d. A 'slate' was kept for those who could not pay. Their names and the amount owing was written down in chalk. All pubs in the villages had tenant landlords who paid a rent to the brewers who were then more numerous than today. This meant a greater variety of ales to drink and a more faithful type of drinker who would stoutly uphold the virtues of his pub landlord's wares. The two pubs in Ascott were owned by different brewers, and there was for years a state of undeclared war between the tenants.

Pub games

Darts usually belonged to the pub and had wooden bodies having a lead belt inset with real feathers trimmed and fixed for flights. Winners took their winnings in half pints of beer, and I have seen as many as fifteen half pints on one broad windowsill waiting to be drunk. Some tried to collect their winnings in tobacco goods but this was frowned upon on account of fluctuating costs. Different brands and the desire of some greedy winners to have 'a large packet' of fags, or an ounce instead of a half-ounce of tobacco, soon put an end to this practice, as these items were generally double the price of a half pint of beer.

Players wishing to have a game of darts put their name on a slate fixed near the dart board, and the winner of each game took on the next name until 'knocked off his perch'. After collecting his darts from the board at the end of his throw, the player threw them point first into the top of the table running alongside the darts pitch. So long a time had this been the practice that this table with its two-inch thick top had a hole about nine inches in diameter chipped out by the points of countless darts. Up to the early twenties some dart boards had the double one divided into two halves.

The playing of 'rings' was dying out fast when I started to go to the pub. A board, usually diamond shaped, had circles drawn about its centre all the same distance from each other. Square hooks were fixed into these circular lines, equal distances apart, and each hook had a number under it. Flat rubber rings of about four inches diameter were lobbed against this board and if any got caught by the hooks the player was credited with the number on the hook or hooks. Smaller editions of this game were played by children at home, and I remember we had one at our house.

There was little music in the pubs those days before the arrival of the juke box. Instead, on a pay night, usually Friday, the landlord would contrive a sing-song with a few drink bribes to the ones he knew would get the show on the move. Sometimes a piano would be wheeled into the bar from the private rooms when a pianist was available to play, and I have had many real good nights taking part in the sing-alongs or listening to some of the old ones doing a solo turn. Although these singers got a lot of stick from their fans, they were well liked both as individuals and for the seldom heard songs from their youth spent in other counties. We had a Mr. Walter Jefferies and his wife who were both good solo pub singers. What a pity there were no tape recorders around at the time as some of their songs I doubt if we shall ever hear again.

Walter's favourite was 'Me Jolly Jolly Old Jacket'; the chorus went like this:

It's all through the beer, the jolly, jolly beer,
It's all through the beer and the baccy,
That's where I spend my tin, with my lassie drinking gin,
And it's across the briny ocean I'll be sailing.

There were many verses to this song, some of which cannot be written down. As Walter had a speech defect which was emphasised by this particular song, he was always being asked to sing it, with the lads joining in. One day in mid-song Walter stopped singing and told his audience, 'Thee bist making a fool outa I, san't sing no more'. It was ages before he could be persuaded to 'give us a song, Walter'.

In some pubs, games such as table skittles and 'tip it' were popular, but they died out in the fifties. Table skittles consisted of a ball at the end of a piece of string attached to the top of a short pole about twenty inches high let into the centre of the left hand side of the table. To the right of this pole, on spots marked on the table in a diamond pattern, stood small skittles about six inches high. The ball would be thrown at the end of its string from the left hand side of the pole and with luck would knock down a few skittles to be recorded in favour of the player. The highest scorer of either a single throw or a set of throws won the game – and the beer.

Shove halfpenny – or 'shove 'appeny' – was, and still is in some pubs, a popular game, although the quality of the boards varied from pub to pub. Some boards were just slabs of polished mahogany with ten parallel lines scored across the top surface. The lines were just over an inch apart. The board should be well polished and have a true plane horizontally. However, damp or neglect would cause the boards to warp out of true, making the outcome of the games often in favour of those who knew the board. The game was usually played by two persons. A worn halfpenny or a brass disc about the same size would be placed over the bottom edge of the board with almost a half of its area hanging in space, the actual point of balance remaining on the board. The player would use the flat of his hand or more particularly the large meaty base of the thumb to strike the disc and send it up the board hopefully to stop within the limits of two lines when it scored one point. This would be marked as a vertical stroke in chalk to the player's side of the board and opposite his disc. When he had done this three times per line, the three chalk marks would be cancelled with a diagonal line. If the disc encroached slightly onto the lines this would cause a lot of argument and sometimes bad humour until the dispute was resolved.

Better boards had brass strips let into the lines, each of which could be lifted and watched to see if it moved a disputed disc. If it did then the claim was not allowed. The game was won when one player had filled all nine lines with three coins each, as shown by the chalk marks on his side of the board. He also won the beer. Some players of this game had exceptional skill in making their halfpennies or discs stop just where they were wanted, or to nudge a disputed disc just that little bit further off a line, so that it scored at the same time that the nudging disc rebounded just enough to remain within its own two lines and also score.

Dominoes is still, with crib and other card games, a popular pub pastime, especially among the older men, some of whom were very skilful players who seldom had to pay for the beer they drank. At the Swan at Ascott there was, before World War II, a landlord by the name of Gardener, whom we have already met. He had a double set of dominoes, and this set is the only one I have ever seen in any pub.

There was a game called 'tippit', or I believe sometimes called 'Pass the piece', which was played by two teams of equal number seated either side of a table or tables. Any equal number of players could in theory play this game but usually there were from eight to sixteen. Each side would choose a captain who would toss a coin for the first go. The 'piece' would be shown to the players; it could be a button or a pea, anything that was small was permitted, and the players sat facing each other. Trying to assume poker faces, with both hands behind their backs, the team with the 'piece' waited to feel their neighbour pass the piece down the line from the captain and back, until the opposing captain called 'tippit' or 'tip it', when the players had to put their clenched fists on the table top.

The captain calling 'tippit' would eye each opposing face and fist and then make his choice by touching or pointing at the fist he thought contained the piece. If he was right, his team scored one and took over the piece for the next game. If he lost the challenge, the other team chalked up one, and so the game

The baseball team in 1922.

proceeded with the next player down from the captain having the next challenge. The game was won when one side achieved the agreed number of
scores.

Just after World War II my brother Cyril who had married a London
evacuee, brought back from London the game of Aunt Sally to the Churchill
Arms and started the vogue for the game which is still going strong.

'Konk' Lewis and the introduction of baseball

In the late twenties there was a revival in the village of the game of baseball, an alleged all-American game. English magazines of that period, which
I have read, credit the game to Chipping Norton where it has always had a
following, and very strong it was in the days of Mr. 'Konk' Lewis, a Chipping
Norton builder and undertaker. He had been to America and was always to
be seen at baseball matches sporting a white Stetson hat, smoking a cigar and
'talking American'. 'Konk' has long since made his last 'home run' but his
memory lingers on. The middle finger on my left hand still has a humped top
joint resulting from the impact of a baseball, which was said to travel at
around ninety miles an hour. The game was played in the field going up to
the top right hand corner of London Lane. I have seen big hitters, such as
Edgar Walton, hit a ball from the batter's base about twenty yards inside the
field gate entrance on the London Lane side, over the hedgerow on the far

side to land on what we call 'New Road', the cart track up from Crown Farm.

Football was also played in this field which was always grass up to the war years and was known as the Football Field. Light aeroplanes sometimes landed there and in the adjacent field. Edgar Walton told me that in World War I a bomber aircraft made a forced landing there. During the second war, and afterwards, until the new playing field was opened up the High Street, this field's activities were transferred to that field now built over by Chestnut Drive and Maple Way Estates.

''Ard on Ernest?'

One of the village characters attended the football matches and walked the boundary line carrying a collection box. This was Raymond Farmer, one of Dad's railway mates who, when seeing a special friend standing watching the game, would go up to him for a chat. Unfortunately, Raymond's enthusiasm for football extended to his feet which followed the feet of the players when they kicked for goal or to clear their area. This meant many a painful kick on the ankle or shins and, as Raymond's boots were of the steel-tipped, hobnailed variety, such a kick was no joke.

Like most railwaymen Raymond was a keen gardener and he loved flowers, especially roses which he grafted on to wild stocks from the hedgerows. Bees, their honey and the bee wine metheglin, were part and parcel of Raymond's life and he could often be seen with his special netted hat and smoke pot collecting bee swarms for his hives. His greeting to my father when they met was a peculiar ''Ard on Ernest?' and Dad would reply ''Ard on, Raymond', followed by 'bloody 'ot ain't it?' or some similar remark. I always thought that this greeting meant 'Hard on!' meaning hard at work, but knowing the dry humour of the ex-servicemen-cum-railwaymen that these men were, it is more than likely that the greeting had a more earthy meaning and was a joke between mates.

Changes at school

At school, Mr. Kinvig was followed as head teacher by a Miss Bucknell, a rather severe spinster who took no nonsense from the older boys who thought she would be easy to manage. They found out differently and had many cane weals on their hands and legs to remind them.

Things changed a bit in the classroom. The Education Committee at Oxford had decided that woodwork would be taught at school, and started off their programme without much thought or preparation. A number of sets of carpenters tools and one carpenter's bench arrived at the school and were dumped in the 'top' classroom, together with a quantity of timber.

No instructor arrived to organise the teaching of woodwork, and after one visit from the 'Organiser for Craft Subjects' stationed in Oxford, Miss Bucknell was expected to teach this new subject on top of her normal work load. The result was chaos; the floor around our desks became covered with wood shavings. The noise of hammering and sawing coupled with the voices of the boys, as they sought to teach each other how to use a saw or plane, made the teaching of the three R's impossible. After two weeks, the tools and bench were sent to Shipton-under-Wychwood where a very large wooden hut had been built in which to teach the pupils away from the ordinary class-rooms. At Shipton, for one half-day per week we were taught woodwork under Mr. Horn, the headmaster of that school. Leafield boys and boys from Milton-under-Wychwood and from Shipton each had a half-day per week learning woodwork until a 'handicraft instructor' was appointed after some long time. It was here, in this environment of a carpenter's shop-cum-class-room, that Mr. Horn persuaded me to try for scholarships and eventually, we hoped, become a teacher of handicrafts.

When Miss Bucknell retired to London she was followed as headmistress by a Mrs. Muir, whose husband was a newspaper editor. She was a hard-working woman determined to improve the quality of education in our school and I'm sure she did. She had one son who attended our school and she treated him rather more harshly than the rest of us; no doubt it was so that she could not be accused of favouritism. I was ill the week she took over the school and when, after a few days off, I made my way to school, she made me take a written examination. What she saw in the result made her latch on to me to cram for the 11+ examination. I remember passing the first part to my mother's pride but failed in the second and most important exam. This second part decided which pupils went to Burford Grammar School, as only so many places were allotted. The invigilators were the school managers, local farmers with children of their own sitting the exam.

I was sure I had passed as I had no difficulty with the questions but my name was not among the list of passes. The children of the farmers passed the exam, and it peeved me a bit as it coincided with the arrival of the *Daily Herald*, the one Labour paper published in the week. Having listened to Dad talking to Mum, and at times to his mates, about the injustices of the times and our poverty, when there was mass unemployment in the land, there started to grow within me that hatred of class distinction and the Tory Party which, because I never disguised it, did me no good in my life but which I shall carry to my grave. My mother, while agreeing with me, was still fearful of the power of the landowners and farmers and cautioned me to watch my tongue in public. 'No good will come of it, Eric, you are too young to understand and they are too strong for us. Walk humble, my son, walk humble.' These words seared into my rebellious mind and I resolved that one day 'they' would pay for their treatment of us.

However, as I passed many more and harder examinations in later years, the bitterness of not going to the Grammar School gradually died down.

At twelve years of age I was attending Shipton Elementary School under headmaster Mr. Horn. He it was who urged me to sit for the Intermediate Exam and then for the first of many handicraft exhibitions, with the view of eventually becoming a handicraft instructor. Each exhibition was worth, at first, £20 per year, rising some years later to £50. Only two were given each year in the county and I won one of them year after year. This meant that I had to attend five different schools per week as I followed the handicraft instructor around his circuit. I was given the use of a cycle for this and had to cycle to Burford while others living a few yards further away were taken there by bus.

At Burford I attended the Grammar School for handicrafts for half a day per week and then again at the Elementary School's new building recently erected in what was then part of the old Grammar School's playing fields.

Homework I received in plenty from Mr. Horn at Shipton, who would give me a full week's homework, and from Mr. Jones of the Burford Elementary School, who would do likewise. Neither of these two teachers was prepared to see that I was doing double the normal load on top of my usual homework on Dad's allotments. This meant that often the only time I could get to do my homework was after everyone had gone to bed at night. Before the electricity was installed in our home I had to do my homework by candlelight or the table oil lamp, and most nights Dad would say, 'Don't sit there all night burning that candle'. I got little encouragement from Dad and had it not been for my mother I would have chucked in the sponge there and then.

Training to be a pupil teacher

When I was fourteen years old, instead of leaving school to find work, I was transferred to Burford Elementary School under Mr. Jones to start my training as a pupil teacher full time. I shall never forget that first week at Burford as a teacher under training and the humiliation I felt at having to stand before the class in clothes obviously not made for me. My jacket was an elder brother's cast-off as were my trousers, and the boots I wore had hobnails in their soles. However, the second week my mother somehow managed to get me a jacket and trousers of better fit and quality and, by prising out the nails from my boots, I felt better dressed and gained more confidence.

There was a change too in my routine as I now had to attend teachers' classes in Oxford all day each Saturday, with a half-day off on Thursday, and I was thus unable to play football or cricket because there was no one to play with on Thursday. The Oxford teachers' classes were held in what was then the Boys' Central School on Gloucester Green, Oxford, which was just at that time changing from a large cattle market to a concrete paved bus station. This station eventually, a few years later, took over this school for its offices.

The classes were composed entirely of female pupil teachers with one exception – myself. Two years later I was joined by a second young male from Chipping Norton. We were instructed for one or two hour periods by a variety of teachers from all over the county and of all ages. Although I rather liked these classes, as for the first time I was able to see the advantages of the secondary and, I suppose, the grammar schools over the elementary schools in equipment and instruction. Here for the first time I had access to a decent (by 1930 standards) chemical laboratory in which to do experiments and to prove my theoretical instruction.

Occasionally a younger male instructor with an eye for the girls would patronise me and cause a few titters among the girls who, I reckon, had got him weighed up anyway. By and large the girls were plain Janes but good natured and honest, and we got along together very well.

We usually went to Woolworths for lunch, if a cup of tea and a bun could be called that. One of the instructors was the bird lover who I mentioned earlier, Mr. Bill Campbell.

I was also given the added burden of having to prepare for gardening exams from the Royal Horticultural Society, and I had to do that homework. To me this was the last straw as I had already got more homework to cope with in preparing lessons and swotting for exams because I still had to fight for my exhibition each year to obtain a little money to exist on. Mr. Jones had an only daughter who had worked at her books so hard that, by the age of 15, she was ready for university to the great satisfaction of her parents who were both teachers. Mr. Jones hoped to do with me what he had done for his daughter and it mattered nothing to him about my obligations to my family with regard to Dad's allotments. Study, study, study was his motto, and he made sure I did as much as I could and often I was at his home after school hours, up to midnight sometimes, being crammed for my exams. What Mr. Jones forgot was that the human brain and body could only take so much and I was getting near breaking point; in fact I had already made up my mind to flop in the gardening field as I could not see the relevance of gardening to a person who was going to teach woodwork – and perhaps metalwork, which had also been thrust upon me. Practical gardening I knew as well as my teachers, and I certainly did not intend to spend time learning the Latin names of plants merely to take an exam I had no use for. Of course I flopped in the exam, and had to endure bitter recrimination from Mr. Jones for so doing. In the end the goodbye to gardening worked to my advantage as I now had more time for my routine work of preparing lessons and giving them under supervision.

Mr. and Mrs. Jones were a very hard-working and conscientious Welsh couple of intense intellectual capacity. There is no doubt that it was Mr. Jones's socialist politics which held him back from rising higher in his profession and in later years he told me of being informed at an interview of this reason for his rejection. The accursed grapevine saw to it that information on Mr. Jones's politics went ahead of him when he applied for other posts. His brilliant university career favoured him not at all.

Had it been left to the Joneses to prepare me for my chosen career I have no doubt that I would have done much better than I did, but the stupid efforts of the Oxford Education Committee to organise my curriculum led to much overwork and frustration for me. The Committee was using me, and I have no doubt others like me, to feel their way into formulating a process of pupil teacher training involving new subjects then coming into the general curriculum, and they were not making a very good job of it.

When I could stand no longer the overload of homework from each of the schools I attended, plus another more elaborate week's homework from the teachers' classes on Saturday, I wrote to the Committee to protest. My letter was not well received by them but the homework was cut to the teachers' classes and the Jones's. This was still more than enough especially if I had to make models to explain parts of the lessons I gave. In the end I took time off from the day work to make these models and fortunately for me Mr. Jones had at last cottoned on to my situation.

The time was approaching when I would have to take the Rural Pupil Teachers' Examination in order to ascertain my fitness or suitability for Teachers' College, and the Oxford Teachers Classes took on a more important role than the other work I did, which did not please Mr. Jones.

A ghost story

While we are with the Joneses I must tell of one small incident which has stuck in my mind for over 65 years, and of which I am reminded each time I pass along a certain stretch of the road leading from Burford to Ascott. Often at the end of the school day I would be given tea by Mr. and Mrs. Jones prepatory to an evening's revision of my work in school and on my preparation for examinations ahead. Sometimes the strictly scholastic atmosphere of these evenings would be interspersed with anecdotes of past history either of Burford and its area or of Mr. Jones's life story.

One bitter winter evening when my lesson had finished early for once and I had been given a 'one for the road' drink of hot blackcurrant cordial, Mr. Jones told me the story of the Dunsden brothers in the nineteenth century. These brothers were local men who indulged in gambling and card playing, not unusual pastimes which still persist, but on this occasion the games led to violence and murder. The brothers were arrested, taken to Gloucester for trial and hanged there. Their bodies were brought back and gibbeted near the scene of their crime. This gibbet tree is still there and the chains in which the bodies were bound and suspended were there until the late 1930s. This tree stands about a hundred yards from the road at the top of Fulbrook Hill near the edge of a wood close to the Old Rough House, itself a scene of murder in the thirties. Mr. Jones went on to say that on nights of a full moon the ghosts of the Dunsdens haunted that stretch of road and sometimes the sound of their ghostly horses could be heard riding the road.

Having finished my drink, I put on my stiff mackintosh coat and my satchel, and said good night. I mounted my cycle for Ascott-under-Wychwood six and a half miles away. As is usual on solo cycle rides at night, my mind fell to roaming over the events of the day, and I pushed my cycle up the steepest part of Fulbrook Hill, in order to enjoy a cigarette. These I sometimes smoked when funds permitted (five Woodbines for 2d). I began to feel the cool breath of the wind which was then rising. At the top of the hill by Waterloo Farm I remounted and started to pedal faster as the hill slackened and I was able to raise my head from the effort of standing on the pedals to push them down. I noticed that the cloud patches were on and off, hiding a full moon which, when exposed, lit up the landscape like daylight, and when cloud rolled over the face of the moon, the wind seemed to blow harder and colder as the night suddenly became darker.

I was approaching the Old Rough House when the hairs on the back of my neck started to rise and I felt suddenly cold under that heavy mackintosh coat. Mr. Jones and his story of the Dunsdens came flooding back to my mind, my legs started to pedal faster, and then I heard it – the sound of ghostly horseshoes hitting the road behind me and coming on faster the more I pedalled. Panic struck me, I looked behind me and saw nothing but still that horse sound came on faster – and faster until I was ready to shriek with fright. There

UNIVERSITY OF OXFORD
DELEGACY OF LOCAL EXAMINATIONS

THIS IS TO CERTIFY THAT

Eric Reginald Moss .... passed the

Examination for Rural Pupil Teachers

in the year 193 *6*, having been examined in the following Subjects:

ENGLISH (Written and Oral), ELEMENTARY MATHEMATICS (including Arithmetic), NATURAL SCIENCE, HISTORY, ~~GEOGRAPHY, FRENCH, MUSIC~~, ART, GARDENING, HANDICRAFT, ~~HOUSECRAFT, NEEDLEWORK~~,

and having passed with credit in the following *four* Subjects:

Natural Science; Art; Gardening; Handicraft.

William C. Burnet.

Secretary of Local Examinations, Oxford.

INDEX NUMBER *64.*

were few cars about in those days and I saw no friendly light coming towards me. I was alone with the devil and I could not see him. Suddenly the moon broke free of those sinister clouds and came out into a large patch of clear sky. It was at that moment that the penny dropped, and I almost sobbed with relief when that hellish horse revealed itself as the tails of my long calf-length, thick, stiff, mackintosh coat, which had flopped against the spokes of my back wheel. Of course the faster I pedalled, the quicker came the clop, clop, clop of the coat tails against the spokes. Lifting my body from the saddle I tucked as much loose coat as I could under my bottom and pedalled home, free at last from my ghostly companion.

Hopes dashed

During the next two years I sat for and passed my City and Guilds Exam in Practical and Theoretical Woodwork, which had not bothered me much as I enjoyed making joints of all kinds, and dovetails elaborated into secret mitre dovetails held no trials for me. It was getting the time to cope with my workload and at the same time trying to satisfy my father that I was pulling my weight on the allotments since the now £50 per year, though welcome, was not paying for my keep now that I was well into my teens and had to be respectably dressed. My eldest brother resented my clothes and the time off from household chores which everyone else had to endure, and it hurt me like a knife thrust when he called me once, in a fit of pique, 'the little gentleman'. Passing exams did not pay bills or bring home the vegetables I ate, and without my mother's support I would long before have abandoned the hope of ever becoming a teacher.

In 1936, one year after passing my City and Guilds Exam, I took and passed my Rural Pupil Teachers' Exam which entitled me to go to a Teachers' Training College. Then, in the last term of 1936, the blow fell which put an end to my plans for becoming a teacher. I was informed by the Oxfordshire Education Committee that they wanted me to go to Loughborough Engineering College, whose fees were £300 per year, one half of which the Education Committee would pay. This left £150 a year for three years for me to find, and amounted to approximately £3 per week. There were no more exhibitions for me to win, so I had no income: my father's total wage was 47/6d per week, far short of the 60/- required, and there was still a family to support of which three brothers were unemployed.

Working at Rissington Aerodrome

In July 1937 I finished my school life and went up to Rissington Aerodrome, then being built, and I got a job as trainee carpenter at 1/- per hour. As re-arming the country made the completion of aerodromes a matter of urgency, I worked most weeks for 52 hours and some weeks seven days per week. I was actually earning more than my father and within six months I was on town rates of pay and getting 1/5d per hour which eventually became 1/7½d per hour.

My health improved, I slept better and ate well, my conscience now clear. I suffered no pangs that I was sponging on my family; indeed I was greatly improving mother's housekeeping money, and she began to sing again.

My work at the aerodrome consisted of cutting and fixing 6 inch x 1inch boards to the roofs of the four large hangars, each roof having one acre of boarding on which green asbestos tiles were fixed. My fellow workers were four ex-Welsh miners on the roof with me, one middle-aged but very active Burford man, Mr. Tom Price, who laboured for us on the roof, and one other middle-aged man named Len who laboured on the ground tying the boards to the rope and pulling them up the 52 feet to his friend on the roof. The boss spent most of his time in the local pubs. These boards were cut to length by us on the ground and handed over to two painters who prime coated them and should have given them two undercoats before they were put on the roof, but this they rarely did if they could get away with it.

As few people relished the vertical climb up the side of the hangar wall via a ladder strapped to this wall, and then walking along bare girders to inspect our work or talk to us, we soon found out that any short cuts in our work we could make were safe from censure once we had the wood laid on the roof members. We were not so fortunate in getting any profit out of our short cuts, unlike the painters who were paid at piece rates. These painters placed our cut boards on two trestles and with one man each end they painted the board towards each other; at the same time they were able to watch both ways for any officious official who might make trouble over the quality of the paint work. Many of those boards had no primer coat and only one undercoat before being hoisted out of harm's way up and onto the roof.

We all had to get to the roof via that ladder which had no protection for our backs. If we slipped on a rung we dropped to the ground – injured. Today there would have to be landing platform every twenty feet plus a back guard against which a body could rest in safety, or a closed lift. In those days it was up the ladder but down the rope. As we all wore wellington boots we grasped both ropes near the pulley and swung our feet so that the rope fed out between our boot soles. One had to watch it as a too fast pace down the rope would burn through the skin or the palms and make them bleed; it also cut grooves in the legs of the wellingtons, and was forbidden under penalty of the sack, but no-one ever noticed since it was a job to get people to work at heights.

When the roofing work finished I went on concrete shuttering work. This was rough and hard on cutting tools as we had to use second hand timber due to the great consumption of wood on concrete work.

The main walls of the hangars between the steel roof support pillars were composed of reinforced concrete poured between joiner-made shutters which were pulled up into place by chain pulleys. If no shuttering oil was put on the shutters the face of the concrete would come off on the shutters and had to be cleaned off before re-use. There were no protective helmets for us or protective boots, men were always walking on nails left in wood thrown on the ground. If a piece of wood was used which had dry knots, these knots would be forced out by the vibrated concrete and liquid concrete would pour to the ground. This meant the sack for the person fixing that wood, and there were always men waiting (to take on these or any jobs) outside the works entrance gates.

Although there were regulations governing the construction of scaffolding, these were often ignored and if a man wanted to keep his job he did not complain. I, together with others, have had to work on bare scaffold tubes because there was a shortage of planks. There is nothing funny about cutting and fixing timber while standing on two-inch tubes with a 50 foot drop below.

One day my friend and I were ordered up onto a bare scaffold to fix some awkward shaped shutters and, as we were closing on the work place, my friend put his foot on a tube from which the clamps had been removed. The tube rolled under my friend's foot and he fell, hitting the protruding ends of the steel putlogs (tubes fixed crossways on steel scaffolding on which planks are placed), before he was able to grasp the last one and swing under it slowing his descent before he hit the concrete floor. To protect himself, the man who had ordered us up on the scaffold told me I would be sacked for going against orders and working on unplanked scaffolding, and that my injured mate would get nothing in money terms from the time he left the site in a car for the hospital. Unions were not encouraged on this site and known union men were not employed, but still the union would surface as it did in this case. While it could do nothing directly for us as we were not members, it did take up the matter of safety with the site management, and its threat to make official protests to the Safety in Management people soon caused a marked improvement in scaffolding.

At about the same time three men were killed on defective scaffolding on similar hangars at Brize Norton, which was being built at the same time.

A dangerous job

Having been sacked from this job, I was immediately offered a job with the painters who wanted help in putting on the last coat of gloss paint on the underside of the planks we had nailed on the roof.

The older of the two painters (the boss) was a foul-mouthed Yorkshire man with blackened teeth and a pipe forever clamped in his mouth. He had been in the business of bridge painting and had no fear of heights.

My first day's work as a painter was the most traumatic I'd had in my young life. To get in place to start painting we had to step on to a single 9 inch by 2 inch plank which was suspended from the steelwork on short 2½ to 3 inch diameter wood poles, with the bark still on them, placed about 12 inches from each end of the plank. These poles were hung from the steelwork by thin single strand wire not more than three-sixteenths of an inch in diameter, and the span between these poles was at least 10 feet with no intermediate support. All scaffold planks were supported every 5 feet by law and here we were, three men, average weight about 9½ stone, complete with galvanised 2-gallon buckets holding 1½ gallons of paint, standing on one plank. The largest brush I had ever used on gloss paint was 2 inches, which is perfectly adequate for normal use. Up here with acres of board to do we had to use 6 inch brushes. A brush of this size loaded with gloss paint was a wrist and arm aching tool as the area of paint spread by the brush had a terrific drag which had to be overcome by brute force and there was no time for fancy brushwork. The old painter saw to it that the paint was flopped on until the undercoat (of a different colour shade) was covered and then the painter moved on. Each movement of the feet caused the plank to swing from side to side, and with the knowledge that there was a 50 foot drop either side of that plank, my time in the roof space was one of nerve-racking horror.

To make matters worse the wood to be painted was sloped towards the painter at an angle of 45 degrees which meant stooping and stretching to do the lower work, while to paint the wood which was almost touching one's face, one had to lean back to allow arm room for the brush.

Had the three painters all painted as one, stooping and reaching at the same time, there would have been a terrible accident. Just as marching troops have to break step crossing bridges, we doing the painting had to paint at different heights and angles to prevent oscillation of that plank which must have bent 6 inches in the centre. To make matters worse for me, that old devil of a painter would deliberately shudder his feet to start the plank swaying while he watched my face with glee. He had the habit, between puffs of his foul pipe, of telling with obvious enjoyment as he watched my face, of the terrible accidents whieh had happened to men while working with him on bridges and other high work. He would then break into singing foul songs as he applied his paint at twice the speed my trembling limbs allowed me to do.

After a week I told the old devil what to do with his paint brushes and left in spite of being offered a rise of 1½d an hour if I stayed on. He had a hell of a job to get painters and when one watched them getting into their overalls at the start of the day's work it was a wonder he got any at all, because the overalls were stiff with dried paint and were stood up waiting to be stepped into.

The steel painters using red oxide paint had a vaseline sheen to their faces and exposed flesh while using their long handled mops to paint the steel. There were few real first class tradesmen working there, just hundreds of poor devils hoping to escape the everlasting dole of 14/- per week for a single man, and to have the dignity of a job and some prospect of feeding his family decently if he was married. Men were sacked for just straightening their backs. A foreman would have a few old hands or his toadies to form the core of his gang to which he added more as the work demanded. When his particular job of the moment was finished, the surplus was sacked, at two hours notice, and they joined the ever-increasing mob at the gates. When the foreman went to the office for his next job he took on extra men sufficient for his task from this gate mob, and the process went on like that ad infinitum.

The pick and shovel gang

Although the urgency of the re-armament made it imperative to have plenty of machines for earth moving, trenching etc., there was alweays need of pick and shovel gangs. Such a gang would be there on the spot at 7 a.m. being spaced out by the foreman at distances apart according to the nature of the ground. Since men worked a normal day up to 5 p.m. with half an hour for lunch, it was not unusual on good ground for the foreman to space his men up to 25 yards apart according to the width and depth of the trench to be dug. At precisely 7 a.m. the thud of the first pick striking earth would be heard, each man having his own shovel with his lunch bag and drink bottle hung nearby. These men picked and shovelled their own stretch of trench and there was little time for talking unless the foreman was away or they were making good progress. In any case very little was said because the foreman would know when he got back how you had worked by the progress made. As said before, a straight back got you the sack.

It was pitiful to see these men when the foreman told them that the job would be finished tomorrow or at latest the day after, and he would have to 'shorten hands', sometimes saying by how many. Men would work twice as hard, hoping to catch the foreman's eye and keep their jobs, but usually the foreman had already made up his mind as to who he was going to lose.

Wartime waste

Waste of material on this site was terrific as Wimpey, the main contractors, with Winston Churchill's money (and influence no doubt) were paid on a cost plus basis and so could not lose. I have seen loads of roof timber, having dozens of lengths of beautiful first class 6 inch x 1 inch prepared one side timber, thrown on to muddy broken roads in order for the lorry to ride over them and get through to its destination. Nails by the hundredweight were wasted or left out in the rain to rust and become useless. In fact I used to fill my pockets with 2½" round wire nails I had swept up in the steel gutters of the roofs or where a sack had split on the ground. These were to come in useful ten years later when I built my own house.

Surplus new 20 inch x 10 inch green asbestos slates, not required by the men putting them on the boards we had fixed, would be tipped over the side with a labourer's shovel, to break fifty feet below, rather than be taken carefully below for re-use elsewhere. These slates had another use. Toilet facilities on the site were either basic pits with no cover, or were non-existent. Few roof workers made the journey down by ladder or rope to use what facilities there were. Urination was onto the side of a roof out of sight; the result would roll into the wide steel gutters between the roofs and mingle with the pools of rainwater resting in the hollows of the long lengths of gutter. Bowel movement was accomplished on a slate laid flat with another laid over the top of the deposit. This sandwich would then be thrown over the side to mingle with the other broken slates on the ground.

The first plane lands

While on the roof of No. 4 hangar, I saw the first aeroplane to land at Rissington, a silver painted Anson and, although an ardent lover of aeroplanes – especially World War I planes – I felt a bit of a let-down as the Anson taxied to within fifty yards of us. The silver coat and the lack of guns in its cupola over the Scarfe ring made it a civvy passenger plane which did not hold much attraction for me. In less than two years I was to have flown 83 hours in Ansons as part of my training. But that story is told in my book, *Solvitur Ambulando*, and we will not bother with it here.

The arrival of the Anson gave an indication as to the aerodrome's progress: buildings were going up everywhere, including a church, and soon I had enough of cycling eight miles in all weathers and uphill to obey the strident order of the Start Work Whistle which could be heard three miles away. Hundreds of very rough Irishmen worked here, but during the Abyssinian Crisis, when it looked as though we might go to war in 1938, they disappeared overnight. I remember cycling across the aerodrome, a forbidden short cut, when I had to stop because of a long deep trench dug for sewerage drainage. As I lifted my cycle over the trench, a rain-sodden, long-haired, bewhiskered face appeared alongside mine, followed by a mud-splattered body. His teeth chattering with cold, the Irishman said, 'Bejabbers bhoy, dem feathers was damn hard last night'. I left him scrambling out of the trench which I have no doubt contained others who had fallen in around midnight on their way home from the Merrymouth – the only pub on that side of the aerodrome for miles. The name, under post-war owners, changed to The Hunter's Lodge with a seven day licence.

Working for Burbidge's

I said goodbye to Rissington to go and work as a joiner for Burbidge's of Chipping Norton. This was a whole new world. No lavish use of nails but the more refined work of making mortise and tenon joints, preparing all timber from the rough and sawing down all planks by hand.

The three Burbidge brothers were gaffered by their eldest member who must have been in his sixties and a strong Chapel man. Like Mr. Andrews and Mr. Willis, mentioned elsewhere, Mr. Burbidge did not believe in modern methods, preferring the time-honoured labours and skills of years ago, now showing the beginnings of a decline as, through necessity, the machine was coming into its own. It sometimes seemed to my young mind that our so-called betters of yesteryear believed in hard manual work for its own sake in a kind of sackcloth and ashes attitude. I could see no real value or sense in spending hours doing hard work for the joy of it when, with a minimum of machinery such as a circular saw and a planer, work could be turned out so much quicker and therefore cheaper, or in another way larger profits could be made.

The Burbidges have now gone, together with Konk Lewis of baseball fame, whose building and undertaking firm were next door; and gone have many of the skills employed by the men who worked for them.

Working on my own account

After some eight weeks with the Burbidges, learning a lot of good sound building knowledge, I was asked to go into business on our own account with a Mr. Longshaw of Ascott. Arthur Longshaw had worked all his life for the Ascott builder and undertaker and he had had enough of the very low wages paid. His wife's father was a butler in a big house at Fifield, below the Merrymouth Inn. He had given Arthur a lot of small building repair jobs to do. Arthur needed help and, as I was attracted by the idea of self employment, not having thought much of the pitfalls, I agreed.

We repainted Ascott vicarage, repaired gutters and renewed wood and stone where necessary. We did work at Fifield Church and built a cart shed there for a tenant farmer.

A family called Jones, mentioned in *Solvitur Ambulando*, gave us some work of repainting, repair and the construction of two flats from three unwanted rooms at the Grange, Ascott. The political news was bad, Hitler was on the march, and we had been building shadow war production factories for some time. We also still had over a million unemployed men and continued to have them well over a year after the war had started.

In the Local Volunteers

The family of Jones were Londoners out to save their skins and expecting, and getting most often, treatment as superior people. Petrol rationing meant nothing to them, they always had plenty and their cupboards were filled with tinned food. I strongly disliked them. Howard Jones, an alcoholic, had been in the army in the first war and, as an ex-lieutenant, he took over command of Ascott's Local Volunteers, as the Home Guard were called when first formed. He had been an engineer of sorts until his addiction to whisky made him incapable of anything except interfering in things which were no concern of his. He and I disputed like Kilkenny cats. I hated his politics, his old-fashioned ideas and his lack of real knowledge of country life hidden by the usual towny know-all attitude. His command of the Local Volunteers was a laugh and the men called him Nodder Jones as his head kept nodding with the alcoholic shakes. We had about four shotguns and six shotgun cartridges, although had an emergency arisen I suspect a few more guns and a lot more cartridges would have surfaced.

When men were detailed to guard bridges or the observation post or the level crossing, Jones had some great difficulty in saying who should go and where he should stand when on guard. He would change his mind a dozen times before he was satisfied and those six cartridges were allocated and re-allocated just as often before the men marched off.

I had a .22 rifle which was accurate to 300 yards and, when I was a P.O.W., I gave it to my youngest brother who loaned it to the Home Guard. So many rounds were fired by this rifle at the butts across the river between the Road and Wooden Bridges, that the Government paid for it to be resleeved and re-rifled. I reckon that little rifle had done its duty for England.

Reporting for duty – and an unexpected gift

The day came when I had to report to the R.A.F. for duty, having enlisted some six months earlier. I had 48 hours notice and I remember the eldest female Jones saying to me when she heard of my going, 'I hope you will finish my work before you go'. Typical – all self and no thought that I might like to spend a few hours at home with mother before I went. Howard Jones the Nodder and I, somehow or other in spite of our many differences, had managed a kind of armed truce and often he came and spoke with me almost as a friend. On the day before I went, I was sent for to see him in his room. When I was inside he wished me well and good luck and said, 'I am going to give you a farewell gift of money, as soldiers never have much. As I have no change I shall have to give you a cheque and, as I could not possibly write a cheque for less than £5, that is what I am giving you. You must understand that, if I had less value in change, that is what you would have had.' A damned old snob to the last; it is a wonder the cheque was not made out in guineas. At least he had given me some thought, which is more than could be said of his sisters.

On 20th July 1940 I became 927023 AC/2 Moss E.R. at No. 23 Egerton Road, Blackpool, where I entered the R.A.F. proper for basic training in square bashing, wireless operation and morse code sending and receiving.

In *Solvitur Ambulando*, Eric Moss describes his World War II service in the RAF as an air gunner in a Blenheim, his crash in North Africa and his capture as a POW. This is followed by his escape and life in rural Italy.

Copies of *Solvitur Ambulando* are available from the author, E.R. Moss, 5 Maple Way, Ascott-under-Wychwood OX7 6AU, price £5.40 c.w.o. by post, or £4.40 if collected (phone 01993 831878).

My Personal Memories

Doris May Warner

Doris (right) and her sister Flo

Doris May Warner (née White) first wrote her memoir in 1964 for a county-wide competition for autobiographical writing. (She added to it later, and this is that enlarged edition.) Of 88 entries, she won first prize.

Doris was born on 10 October 1904 and died on 28 November 1986.

Our thanks are due to Harvey Warner for helping provide photographs and additional background information.

My Personal Memories

When I was a small child a visiting Vicar from the dockland slums of Portsmouth preached us a sermon on 'Truly your lot hath fallen in a pleasant place'. It made a lasting impression on me and often as I have roamed the fields and forest, or cycled the lanes, I have remembered and repeated that text, and been glad it has been my lot to have been born and lived in this 'Pleasant Place', Ascott-under-Wychwood, as many generations of my family have been before me.

One of my earliest recollections is of my father getting me out of bed one summer's night and carrying me up the lane to watch Halley's Comet. My father was very keen on astronomy and music, a choir man and bellringer for forty years. He was a shoemaker, a craftsman, and although a cripple, took part in all the village activities, and loved a joke and a laugh. My mother was a pretty, slim, quiet person with a lovely complexion, often ill, and worked to death making two very short ends meet, keeping the house spotless, and making all our clothes. They were married when Dad was an apprentice earning twelve shillings a week, and although they never had owned much they were always ready to give to others in need, and were one of the happiest couples I have ever known.

There were we three children, one son and two daughters. My mother's sister, Aunt Jane Kilby, was the village midwife, nurse, and 'layer-out' so we heard a great deal of birth and death as a matter of course.

I started school at the age of three years. It was a Church of England school. Two rooms as it still is; the 'Big Room' where Mr. Kinvig and Mrs. Kinvig taught the older children, with a pupil teacher sometimes too, and the 'Infants' room, where Miss Perkins and a pupil teacher taught the three to six year olds. There were around 80 to 90 children altogether, about 30 infants and 60 in the Big Room. Mr. Kinvig was a neat small man, a fine man – he came from the Isle of Man so naturally was called 'Kelly'. He gave us good grounding in all the general subjects, at least we could read and write before the age children start school now. The boys had an allotment and had gardening lessons while the girls had sewing and knitting lessons. We had plenty of music and singing, and the Vicar, the Rev. C. Walford came often to school.

We went to Sunday School before Church on Sunday morning, and Sunday afternoons we often went to the Vicarage gardens after classes. We had a Sunday School party in the summer and a Christmas party after the Prize giving. There was an Ascott Charity (and still is) that gave money to buy books for the school prizes. (Also they buy coal at Christmas for all widows and old persons.) The row of houses by the Church used to belong to the Charity. Now they have been sold and the interest on the investments is used for these charities. My greatest friend at school was Kit Ferriman who lived at Kingstanding. In the holidays we roamed the Forest and Common and were so happy. Then terrible tragedy came to her. Her mother died suddenly, then her father was killed by a young horse at harvest time. So Kit and her three brothers were adopted by their neighbour.

Then a great change came for Ascott. Mr. Reginald Tiddy came to live at Priory Cottage with his father and brother, and Mr. and Mrs. Sanderson Furniss had Chestnut Close built. Mr. Tiddy had the Hall built for Morris and Country Dancing and all the young folks learned to dance. Mr. Kinvig was very keen and we learnt at school until the Hall was finished. Mr. Cecil Sharpe often came to Ascott collecting old folk songs and dances. My sister had a shilling for singing to him. He borrowed my grandfather's, William Honeybone's, Morris bells from my mother, and William Kimber copied them for Morris teams. I still treasure these bells and like to think of my grandfather dancing with them over a hundred years ago, and of them being handled by Cecil Sharpe, William Kimber and Reggy Tiddy – three men who gave so much happiness to others. My Aunt used to tell me grandfather and the Morris team used to dance at Cornbury Park and the big houses at Whitsun and the maids who brought out the refreshments for them some-times put 'jallop' [something stronger!] in their beer.

Soon the Ascott country dancers were in great demand at fetes, flower shows etc. and we have had many lovely times out dancing at lots of places such as Bruern Abbey, Abbotswood, Cornwell Manor, Lower Slaughter Manor, Shipton Court, Lee Place etc. etc. The women were busy making the dresses – the adults had dresses with a tight bodice and full skirt, white spotted muslin dutch bonnets and fichus, their hair in two long plaits with ribbons on hair and shoes to match their dresses. The men had white flannels with coloured baldrics, and bells on their legs. The children had coloured flowered-print dresses and matching sunbonnets for the girls, and holland smocks with wide hats and red scarves for the boys. Mr. Furniss (later Lord Sanderson)

Top: The Ascott Country Dancing Troupe at Lee Place, Charlbury, 1925.
Bottom: The Flamborough Sword Dance.

used to play his fiddle to accompany the Morris dances and jigs, although he was blind.

Mr. Tiddy had a bathing place made in the river for the boys with a hut and diving board etc. but the floods kept washing them away. Mrs. Furniss then started a Margaret Macmillan Clinic at the Tiddy Hall. There were three doctors attended. Dr. Parsons from Shipton and Dr. Croly and Dr. McNeight from Charlbury and two nurses lived in the village They also started the May Homes at Stoneliegh for people from London who needed a holiday. The schoolchildren in turns went to the clinic Saturday mornings. There was also a dentist, so we had our teeth attended to and were weighed and examined by the doctor and had treatment whenever necessary. Adults had treatment for a small charge. The Hall was built up on brick pillars about two feet from the ground to give more spring to the Morris dancing, so when it was the turn of the doctor who scared me, I crawled right in under the Hall where no one could find me! But usually we loved the Clinic and the exercises.

The W.E.A. classes

In 1913 Mr. Albert Mansbridge came to stay with Mr. Furniss quite often and they started the W.E.A. here. My brother was the first secretary until he went away at the age of 16 to work on the Railway. Then my sister was secretary for a good many years until 1936. We had women's classes in the afternoons and mixed classes in the evenings once a week, and lots of 'socials' where everyone danced and sang. There were 120 members of the W.E.A.

Ascott fete 1939 with Mr and Mrs Oliver Watney and Rev and Mrs W. Bartlett.

and amalgamated Folk Dancers. The W.E.A. was kept alive here for 30 years; we were the oldest rural class in the country and managed to keep going through both wars, and the years between. Eventually, I regret to say, the W.E.A. was pushed out, so the W.I. could be pushed in. It was a great pity after all the years of effort to keep going. During the years we had many fine lecturers who have later become very well known. The first women's lectures were given by Mrs Furniss and Mrs. Mary Stocks, now well known on radio programmes. I remember Dr. Reginald Jaques giving us community singing, Mr. Barrett Brown of Ruskin, Mr. Lower and Mr. Allan Bullock history lectures just before the War – and many others now well known including Professor Mackay.

In 1911 it was a very hot summer and a drought; all through the long blazing summer holidays the water carts came to pump water from our well for Fairspear High Lodge and Kingstanding. Ascott is well blessed with water: the main supply comes from the Vicarage springs just about a hundred yards up the hill from our house. It was lovely sparkling ice cold water, but it's not the same now it has been piped and tapped and messed around with. Many cottages used to have their own wells in the gardens, but they are nearly all filled in now.

The Vicarage ghost

There used to be a ghost at the Vicarage. It was the ghost of Miss Tweed, sister of a former vicar. (I see in my old Deanery magazines that Rev. Robert Tweed was Vicar here in 1861 so she wasn't a very ancient ghost!). She would appear in the small bedroom over the scullery, look in a big cupboard, and then disappear. My grandmother, Mary White, saw her many years ago, and Miss Cox, a neighbour, saw her. Then Miss Grepe, the Rev. C. Shackleton's sister-in-law, saw her, so Mr. Shackleton held a service of exorcism and I've never heard of any further appearance. Only last year they made a new flat of that room and I wondered what happened to 'Miss Tweed's cupboard'.

The Vicar used to run a clothing club. He used to take the money, 6d or 1/- a week, at school on Mondays, then there would be so much to the £1 added and it could be drawn out at Christmas. I remember walking to Charlbury with my mother to spend it.

Many women 'did the gloving' by hand in those days. Several brought their bundles of gloves, tied up in red and white big handkerchiefs (known locally as bundling hankechers) to my father's shop to be called for by the carrier's cart. This cart went from Leafield to Chipping Norton twice a week, driven by a remarkable couple, Temp and Trump Collicut. They had a big roan horse and a high dog cart that rocked like a boat on the tide. Temp (short for Temperance) had a remarkable flow of language and peculiar sayings, such as 'Master White, thee tell that ther ooman as they aint got none so the'll keep it till Wednesday'.

I remember seeing Mr. Lloyd George go by as he came up from the station to open the Leafield Wireless Station (now Oxford Radio) about 1912. I remember on summer nights sometimes we could see the 'Phantom Lights', the 'Jack O' Lanterns' dancing in the fields up on Chippy Hill.

Altogether I had a very happy childhood. We had very few toys and very rarely a penny for sweets; a new book at Christmas, but we were very happy country dancing and roaming the fields and forest. Then came 1914 and war was declared.

The first world war

My recollections of the War are mostly of the 'King's Liverpools', the soldiers who were guarding the Wireless Station, and a right rum lot they were, mostly Liverpool Irish who seemed to speak a different language. My father had to mend their boots – endless sackfuls of big army boots, from early morning to late night. Then there were the 'wireless operators' – dashing young men in naval uniform – several married local teachers. Mr. Kinvig and several young lads, 'the Volunteers', guarded the pumping station at Coldwell Brook.

We children used to pick blackberries and hips for the Forces. By the time we had been all over the Common gathering them, then we would have to take them from Ascott school to Shipton school to be weighed in, we would have walked 10 or 12 miles and earned a 'certificate' for war work. Food got very short. One week I remember we only had 2 oz. of pastry lard and nothing else for all the family. We lived mostly on vegetables and fruit and home cured bacon, and the only sweets we had were awful black hard things called locust beans, or a bit of chewing gum.

Then a sad thing for Ascott. On 11th August 1916 Mr. Tiddy was killed in action. 14 Ascott men lost their lives in the War.

A few more pre-war memories occur to me. I remember the gas being brought to Ascott and the gas lights and stove being installed (about 1910). Also I can just remember my father going to the last meeting of the Court Lete, the ancient kind of parish council that used to be held annually at the Churchill Arms to arrange parish affairs. One of the most exciting things for us during the war were the visits we had from our overseas cousins in the Forces from Canada and Australia My brother was married at the age of 20 on his only leave from France.

Leaving school at 13

When I was 13 I had to leave school and start work at Dee's Stores at Shipton-under-Wychwood. For the large sum of 4/- per week I had to work 52 hours per week and also walk 4 miles a day. The hours were 9 a.m. to 6 p.m. Monday, Tuesday and Thursday, 9 a.m. to 1 p.m. Wednesdays, 9 a.m. to 7 p.m Fridays, and 9 a.m. to 8 p.m. Saturdays, which was often 9 p.m – especially at Christmas. No closing for meals so I often might start dinner at 12 and perhaps finish it at 3 as I always had to serve while the others had their meals in peace. Of course it was a big help to have din ner and tea allowed while food was so short. It was a very busy shop and I learnt a great deal there dealing with grocery, drapery, chemistry, millinery, hardware, men's outfit-ting, boots and shoes, window dressing etc. I had to learn it all.

During the winter they used to have two pigs in every fortnight which made a lot of work. Very often the cottagers would pay for the year's grocery bills with one pig and draw cash for the other one. A good many people had

Left to right: Gwen Baylis, Alf Tilling and Doris White.

to pay for half their living with the money they made on their pigs. Besides selling the pork and curing the bacon and hams, they used to make sausages, lards, scratchings etc. There were two sisters and two brothers in the family, most upright straightforward good people, and they taught me a great deal. Then Mr. Dee married the other assistant. He was 62 and she was 26, so it made a lot of excitement. Then Miss Mary Dee fell down dead in Church.

I remember on 11th November 1918 I was sent to stand at the bootroom window upstairs with a huge Union Jack and told to keep my eyes on the Post Office, and the second they put their flag up I was to unfurl ours. The next day I was ill with that awful flu that swept the country. It was very bad here. Eight people died of it. We had a new Vicar just come to the village at that time, the Rev C. Shackleton. Our old Vicar, the Rev C. Walford, had been injured when helping to fell a chestnut tree in the Churchyard, and he never recovered – he was such a kind, gentle old man. Mr. Shackleton tended the sick people and looked after families who had no one to help, as so many people were ill.

Music and dance

The Shackletons were such a happy-go-lucky family, very musical, and joined in everything that happened in the village. It made such a difference to the life of the village when they were here. They had a lot of foreign students too who all joined in with everything. The Tiddy Hall was a great part of village life then. Beside the W.E.A. lectures and folk dancing, every week we had whist drives and socials, concert parties, Boy Scouts and youth clubs etc. besides special events of all kinds. The country dance team often gave displays at local fetes etc. My sister taught folk dancing at a class at Lower Slaughter, a very pretty village about 12 miles away, just over the border in Gloucestershire, and got engaged to a young man there. A very pleasant friendship grew up between the two villages, our football teams, concert parties etc. exchanged visits and we went to each other's dances etc. It was all good fun while it lasted.

After Mr. Dee and Miss Dee had died the business was sold to Mr. Rex Hathaway who had just come out of the army. Life was very different then! Instead of Miss Dee's large joints and family size pies and cakes etc it was stewed rhubarb and half a sheep's head for dinner! When I was 21 I left Hathaway's and we took over the Post Office at Ascott. For the large sum of £4 per month we were open from 9 a.m. to 7 p.m., no dinner hour closing.

The mail came at 6 a.m., we were sorted and out on delivery at 7 a.m. The letters went out by train at noon and another mail in by train too. The last collection was at 8 o'clock at night and went out on the 8.30 train, so it was a long day. It was some years before the mails all came by motor mail vans. My father had to walk up to Kingstanding and High Lodge, then across to Fairspear and Langley and the Radio Station right out to the Meteorological Office. Sometimes he would come home with blood and matter coming through the lace holes of his boots from his bad foot, so eventually he had to give up the round and Jim Chandler our neighbour took it on. I delivered down to Ascott Mill every morning, and Mary Edginton delivered the village. When she finished after over 40 years service, Nelly Trinder delivered the village mall.

I should think there is no place like a village post office for learning all about one's fellow creatures. Whether it is the state of their poor feet, their internal organs, or their most secret love life, you had to stand and hear it all, there is no escape! I used to hear such tales from Old Age Pensioners too of the old days, especially from one old man, Jacky Pratley, a retired shepherd well over eighty. He could remember when the Forest was cut down when it grew nearly to the Charlbury Road and the tramps and wanderers had to work in the village saw pits belonging to the Cornbury Estate before they could spend a night in the workhouse, which used to be in the houses between the Church and the Green. If you told him the date and time of the changes of the moon, he would give you a weather forecast more accurate than any BBC. He would say, 'Ah my wench, I be the King of Ascott, and Her up at the Top thinks as hers the Queen' – 'Her' being Mrs. Chaundy of Yew Tree Farm who was on most committees etc. He used to tell me tales about my grandfather William Honeybone who with George Beachamp were the first men to drive a threshing machine in this district, then Mr. Beachamp's smock got caught in the machinery and he was drawn into the engine and killed – and tales of my grandmother Eleanor Honeybone who was known as 'Lovely Eleanor'.

We had a lot of fun in those days, our house seemed to be always full of people who were practising or rehearsing something for the Church Choir or the concert party or socials. As my sister played the piano and Church organ and sang alto, and my father had a good bass voice, we always had plenty of music and singing. We worked hard and we played hard especially at Christmas time. For ten days before Christmas the mails would arrive at 4 a.m! It was a rush to be sorted and back from delivery by 9 a.m. Hard on all day in the office, then out Carol singing with the Choir for St Dunstan's till 10 p.m. We always had a big Christmas provision Whist Drive before Christmas. Boxing Day we would be busy making our fancy dresses and decorating the Tiddy Hall ready for the following night which was our big

The post office at Ascott-under-Wychwood between the wars.

event, the invitation Fancy Dress Dance. The Hall would be crowded with friends from all the surrounding towns and villages; everyone looked forward to that night, we always had a good time. New Year's Eve would be the choir and ringers' party; then in January we went to Dr. Croly's dance at Charlbury.

We were all dancing mad at that time and went in for competitions and had good bands at the Hall – took it really seriously. The boys had a very good baseball team. We often went out to matches at Chipping Norton, Banbury or Birmingham with them. I bought a racing bicycle, the first in the district and we had lovely rides for miles around. My friends would ride some distance behind me going through the villages to hear the remarks the people made. 'Our Side' as we called ourselves was a lively little crowd and we had a lot of fun with dancing, cycling, motor bikes etc. Saturday nights we could go to Oxford by train for 1/3 - now it's 5/6. So we often went to the theatre or cinemas, or folk dance parties at the Town Hall, or sometimes a W.E.A. Social at Ruskin College or a W.E.A. Summer School at Rhodes House. We also did quite a lot of boating on the river at Charlbury, Oxford, or Radcot Bridge, until I fell out of a canoe at Stratford and wasn't so keen any more.

In 1929 my father died of cancer at the age of 58. It was a cruel death for such a kind man and all the village mourned his loss. My sister had just gone to live at Kidlington, so my mother and I had a quiet life until she died too in 1937.

The second world war

Then I lived alone for nine years. In 1937 I was the Secretary for Coronation Celebrations Fund. As my father was Secretary for the Diamond Jubilee Celebrations in 1897 and I was again Secretary for the Coronation Celebrations in 1952, it is interesting to compare the accounts for the three events. (Cannot find the accounts for the Diamond Jubilee but have found accounts for the 1911 Coronation). Talk about the 'Good Old Days'! When the whole village could have a real feast for £28. 253 lbs. of meat for under £9! Apparently Coronation mugs that cost about 6d. each are now fetching up to 25/- each in antique shops.

When war broke out we had an influx of evacuees, mostly children from East Ham – about 50 schoolchildren besides mothers with babies and private evacuees. For days many of the children just sat on the grass bank outside the

Post Office waiting for a letter from 'our Mam' but when they started school they soon got used to village life.

The office was open Sundays and all times, there was so much to do. Endless forms to be delivered and filled in; Civil Defence instructions, gas masks instructions, ration books, clothing coupons, billeting orders etc. etc. Ascott station was the centre for the unloading of bombs. They were stacked all along the roads, a pile every 12 yards along the main roads, Charlbury to Burford and Chipping Norton to Shipton. They were great big ones, and smaller ones were piled along the roads into the village. It was creepy to walk along the lanes in the twilight between these tons of bombs and wonder where they were destined to drop and how many poor souls they would destroy. The Americans had an office in a hut at the top of the lane and their bomb lorries rumbled by day and night.

When there were War Weapons Weeks and Savings Weeks I went with Dr. Scott to fetes etc. at surrounding villages which had no Savings Bank facilities and sold Savings Certificates, Bonds, Stamps etc. and took Savings Bank deposits etc. there. One special Savings Week we had had Whist Drives etc. for Certificate prizes and I'd attended several fetes for Savings Bank work and finished up Saturday night with over £8,000 in the house, so it shook me when I got up Sunday morning and found I'd forgotten to lock the doors when I went to bed.

All in the corset of duty

Well, all the big events are in the history books, but it's the funny little personal episodes one remembers now. Like the stately 'lady' evacuee who came in the office one day and asked for a Savings Bank withdrawal. I gave her the withdrawal notice and asked for her Bank Book. She said it was not convenient, so I said I couldn't give her the money unless I had made the withdrawal in her book. So much to my surprise she bent over, put her head on the counter and said, 'Then will you kindly put your hand down my back and get my book out of the pocket in my corsets'! So we went into my living room and practically undressed her before we could reach the book with her identity card etc. in her safe hiding place. I often wondered how she managed in a busy city office.

One of my favourite recollections; we were coming up the road from the funeral of a neighbour, Mrs. Trinder, and I was walking with another neighbour, dear old Miss Cox, when we heard a banging over the Radio Station. 'Coo, Thunder,' she says, and stuck her head under my coat quite terrified, then peeped out and said, 'Oh, it's only them Germans,' and scrambled up the

COMPARISON OF ACCOUNTS FOR CORONATION CELEBRATIONS HELD IN ASCOTT UNDER WYCHWOOD IN 1911, 1937 & 1952

	1911	1937	1937	1952	1952
Total Expenditures:	£28. 13. 9		£25. 18. 0		£103. 17. 4
Meat	(40lbs Ham, 68½ Salt Beef, 62½ Mutton, 82½ Roast Beef) 8. 19. 5	(13 Topside Beef @ 1/- / 13 Silverside @ 11d / 62 Ham @ 1/3)	5. 3. 6	Pork, Ham & Tongue	26. 0. 0
Bread	70 Loaves @ 5d 1. 9. 2	10 Loaves @ 9d.	7. 6	10 Loaves @ 8d	6. 8
Beer	45 Gallons 1. 16. 0	14 Gallons	1. 16.10	18 Gallons	7. 16. 0
Potatoes	2½ Cwt. 1. 7. 0				
Puddings	80 lbs 2. 0. 0				
Cheese	6 lbs 4. 3		5. 5	Cider and Lemonade	10. 10. 0
Minerals	36 dozen 1. 4. 0		1.10	6 Gallons Cider	1. 8. 0
Salt & Mustard	1. 8				
Tables	1. 10. 0				
Table Cloths	1. 6. 0				
Childrens Teas	2. 0. 0				
Sports Prizes	4. 0. 0	53 Prizes	5. 0. 0	Sports Prizes	10. 0. 0
Sundries	2. 16. 3	1 Tea	2. 6	Cut Loaves	10. 7½
		12 Loaf Sugar @ 3d	3. 0	Cakes	5. 0. 0
		10 Butter @ 1/2	11. 8	400 Fancy Cakes	5. 0. 0
		Sauce	3. 0	2 Boxes Tomatoes	2. 14. 0
		Milk	3. 0	Ice Cream	2. 0. 0
		Slab Cake	14.11	Grocery	6. 5. 7
		Small Cakes	19. 7	Radio Amplifier	6. 6. 0
		5 doz Mugs	15. 12. 9	9 doz Mugs @ 23/- per doz	10. 7. 0
		Childrens Teas	1. 8. 5	Draw Books	1. 0. 0
		Evening Party at Hall	2. 10. 0	Cheque Book	5. 0. 0
		Flags & Sundries	4. 10. 0	2 Seats were bought with remainder of cash in hand	
			1. 16.10		
	£28. 13. 9		£25. 18. 0		£95. 8. 10½

bank and cheered on the planes shooting at the German plane as they fought and brought it down. One day a German plane dropped a stick of bombs right across Ascott, but providentially, by being a split second too soon, each bomb dropped just a yard or two short of a house so not much damage was done, until one of the last bombs fell on the barn where my fiancé and the men had just unloaded a load of corn. They had just gone back to the fields, but all the corn and the barn was burnt out.

One Christmas when things were getting very short, my friend Mrs. Cox and I collected a lot of old toys etc. and smartened them up, and I sold them in the office and made nearly £40 for the Red Cross. We joined the Civil Defence and learnt first aid, etc. Ivor was in the Home Guards. There was so much work to be done always. One night in the September when invasion was expected it was nearly dark when several lorry loads of Guardsmen (they were stationed at Bruern Abbey) drew up outside. They lined up, then sat down on the grass all around the house. I looked out of the window and asked what was going on. The officer said, 'All strategic points have to be guarded tonight'. I said I'd never been called that before. He said, 'Actually, it's the telephone and all lines of communication to be guarded' (all this was whispered). So when I went to bed, through each window I could see long legs stretched out and big boots sticking up – it looked so funny. They went off at 3 a.m. and the invasion never happened!

Then some 'Pioneer' troops were billeted in the Tiddy Hall, they were unloading coal lorries at Ascott station.

They usually had a dance every Friday night for the villagers as we could not have the use of the Hall for anything else. These dances were usually arranged by one of the soldiers who I was surprised to find I had met at a holiday camp at Dovercourt just before the war. Then he was one of the dashing young men at the camp, in white flannels who organized the sports and dances. Now he is a well known actor often on T.V., Mr. Bill Owen.

My mother's voice

One incident I shall never forget happened to me about 1940-41 in that very cold hard winter; it proves that those who have gone on can still care for and help those left behind. My mother had died in 1937. One Monday night I was sitting in my living room doing my Post Office accounts, actually adding a long column of figures in the Postal Order Stock Book, so I was quite wide awake. Suddenly my mother's voice spoke from the chair where she always used to sit. She said, 'Doris – I wish you would go up in the attic and find my new vests out of the big black box then send them to your Aunty Polly at

Doris in the floods on Whit Monday, 1935.

Folkestone. She is in such a bad way and she has got nobody to help her.' I said, 'Alright Mum, I'll find them right away,' which I did, and not until I had done that and written to my Aunt did I realize what a strange thing it was had happened. My Aunt wrote back and said her street had been badly shelled and she was the only one left living in it, all the other people had been evacuated, but she would not go although she was crippled, and that was just like Kate – always helping people still. My mother also spoke to my sister when I was very ill in hospital in 1946, and asked her to help me.

Married and a baby

When the war was nearly over I gave in my notice to the Head Postmaster. I had had no holiday for 12 years and was feeling quite worn out and felt it was time I thought about myself and my future. So in March 1945 I retired from the Post Office after 19 years service. The people were very kind to me, and presented me with a nice writing table and the school children gave me large blue vase. For the next few months I was busy doing up my house and sewing for a Church fete, and making my wedding dress and suit and the bridesmaids' dresses.

On 29th September, 1945, Ivor and I were married at 5.30 p.m. on a Saturday afternoon. The Church was decorated for Harvest Festival so it was a real farmer's wedding. Everything looked so lovely with the evening sun shining through the Church windows. The Church was packed and all the old Choir members and ringers came and helped to make it a lovely service. We had a party at the Tiddy Hall afterwards, and it was really a grand gathering of friends from everywhere who had not met all through the war, so everyone enjoyed it. We wandered around in the car for a few days, down to Bournemouth.

By the next summertime I was attending Clinic at the Radcliffe with my card marked 'Twins – Queried?'! Then on 2nd October I was admitted to the hospital with toxaemia, oedema, allergic blood and about everything else one can have at these times.

My long stay in hospital completely changed my outlook on life. It was a different world to me. Not only one's own troubles, but all the things others were going through were unforgetable, and above all, the lack of privacy and darkness –

From the Chipping Norton Deanery Magazine, no. 682, November 1945.

ASCOTT-UNDER-WYCHWOOD.

A Michaelmass Wedding. It was the wedding day of a girl whom everyone knows and everyone loves, so everyone was there to wish her and her partner happiness. It was Michaelmass Day, and Harvest Festival was on the morrow. Ascott's Church was stacked with ripe fruits and corn sheaves, and gay with the gorgeous blooms and foliage of autumn. Candles gleamed from the Chancel and on the great candelabrum in the Nave. The congregation filled the building, flooded with light from the unseen host on guard. The Minister and clerks waited in the ancient porch through which so many brides and grooms have passed, down its 800 years of history. Singing the nuptial hymn, the procession moved to the Chancel step. The beautiful service of Holy Matrimony proceeded reverently to its climax, when the couple, kneeling before the altar, received the final Blessing. While a hymn was being softly sung, the Vicar gave the couple God's Message of pastoral counsel and cheer. Soon came the triumphant notes on the organ of the wedding march, and the bridal retinue moved out into the glorious sunshine, and down the churchyard path between the ranks of friends and neighbours in the time-honoured way. As they went along, the old rooster up on Ascott's Norman Tower, turned slowly round on his perch, and made a deep and solemn bow towards the happy pair. It was not every day that a bride was seen among our Parochial Church Council ! No one seemed to notice him, as quite naturally they were all looking at Ivor and Doris Warner as they stepped out together into a brave new life, followed by the sincere good wishes of their many friends, happy in the knowledge that they will have them among them in their **married home.**

how I longed to be in the dark, but there were always lights burning some-where. Also I was so tired of being surrounded by students and doctors and being lectured about because I had so many things the matter; it seemed as if one ceased to be a human being, and was just a 'specimen' for examination and lectures and X-rays etc. I was 42 that month so was considered a kind of freak to be having my first baby, apparently. Anyhow, we stuck it out the full time and on 22nd November I had a Caesarean operation and my baby was born a lovely boy, 7lbs. 12 oz., so it had all been worthwhile.

We were home in time for Christmas – I'd thought I'd never be home again. It was that terrible winter with deep snow, we were shut in. We did not get out with the pram until March, then they cut a path out so we could go to a wedding. It was a very different life, to be minder of a baby after always being in business. But the years flew by and in no time Harvey was at school and growing up so fast.

'Over the Hills to Glory'

In 1952 I was secretary and treasurer for the Coronation funds. So at last I was able to do what I had wanted to do for years, but never had time to do. For years I had felt that the Ascott Martyrs wanted me to tell their story, and I had collected stories from the old folks about the sixteen women of Ascott who were sent to prison in 1873 for stopping Ramsden men who had not joined the Agricultural Workers' Union, who were coming to take the work of Ascott men who had been sacked for joining the Union when Joseph Arch was here.

So I wrote a play telling the story, and called it *Over the Hills to Glory*, that being the name of a country dance with a very catchy tune which we had for our signature tune; and going 'over the hills' to the old folks meant being sent to Chipping Norton to the prison or the workhouse.

As far as possible all the actors were descended from or connected with the characters, and the scene was set in my grandmother's cottage in the Row. We had a lot of fun doing it, twice at Ascott and at Shipton and Churchill. The money we raised was divided between the Coronation funds and the folk dance funds. Mr. Baylis of Oxford who was a reader at the Bodleian Library kindly helped me a great deal by obtaining a copy of newspapers of the time so I was able to get all details correct.

Strangely enough, only a few weeks ago my neighbour showed me a letter in the newspaper asking for information about the Ascott Martyrs for the Chipping Norton Trades Council. So I got in touch with the Secretary and gave them the story and press cuttings which they say will be sent to the

'Trades Union, Labour Co-operative Democratic History Society, Sussex, and placed in their Records for exhibition purposes with other treasures' – so at last 'the Women' really will have gone 'Over the Hills to Glory'!

In case you are interested in the story, here it is, as told in the newspapers of the time:

'Rioting in Chipping Norton! Sixteen Ascott women sentenced to hard labour! Police re-inforcements were sent to Chipping Norton to deal with a crowd of rioters who attacked the Police Station and attempted to rescue 16 women of Ascott.'

The trouble started when Mr. Hambidge of Crown Farm, Ascott sacked his men who had joined the Agricultural Workers Union and then employed men from Ramsden to do his hoeing. The Ascott women stopped these men from working, and tried to persuade them to join the Union. The women were arrested, taken to Chipping Norton, and charged with obstructing and coercing John Hodgkins and John Miller with a view to inducing them to leave their employment on 20th May. The two magistrates conducting the trial were Rev. T. Harris and Rev. W. E. Carter. Mr. Hambidge engaged a solicitor (Mr. Wilkins) to conduct the prosecution but the women were not defended by counsel. The magistrates pleaded with the farmer not to proceed with the prosecution, as they would have no option but to send the women to prison. This he refused to do. So the ringleaders were sentenced to imprisonment with hard labour, seven for ten days, and nine for seven days. When the sentence became known to the public there was a great uproar, and by 9 p.m. there were over 1000 infuriated people swarming around the police court. They tried to rescue the women and broke the windows of the police court and the street lamps. Mr. Holloway of the Workers Union, the Mayor of Chipping Norton Mr. Rawlinson, and Alderman Farwell, endeavoured to quieten the rioters without success. The violence continued until 11 p.m.

The women were taken into two dark rooms with very few seats so they were obliged to take turns in resting. Here they were kept until 1 a.m. an hour after the crowds had dispersed at midnight. A telegram for police re-inforcements had been sent to Oxford. When these arrived in a four horse dray the women were transferred to the drays and set out thus, through the cold night on their journey to Oxford prison. They had no warm clothing but huddled together for warmth and tried to protect the two small infants with umbrellas. They arrived at Oxford at 6 a.m.

They were given washing and ironing to do for their labour, excepting the two women with infants who were excused from working. (Eight of these women were single, and eight married). During their enforced absence their children were at first cared for by kind neighbours and officials of the Milton under Wychwood branch of the Workers Union. They are now in charge of the Ascott Workhouse.

The next day a big meeting of protest was held in Chipping Norton when a crowd of 3000 was addressed by Joseph Arch. The following resolutions were passed, to be presented in Parliament:

1. An extension of the franchise
2. A repeal of the Criminal Law Amendment Act
3. Appointment of stipendiary magistrates

A collection was taken in aid of the women of Ascott. £80 was subscribed (£5 in coppers). 'We understand that questions are to be asked in Parliament and that a personal appeal to Her Majesty Queen Victoria is to be made on behalf of the Ascott women, and therefore trust that justice will be done, and these unfortunate women set free'.

Eventually the Queen granted them all a free pardon, and sent them each 5/- and a red flannel petticoat. Joseph Arch and the Union gave them each a new blue frock and £5 when they came home and received a big welcome and dinner and had their photos taken. I have often thought what a marvellous film could be made of this story – in fact I sent the play to the Ealing Studios in 1956 but they said they were just doing a film about the Tolpuddle Martyrs, so it would be too similar.

Holidays

In 1957 my Canadian cousins Ben and Dorothy Howell came to England for the summer and from May till October they made our house their head-quarters in between trips to the Continent and all around the country, so we had quite a time. But Ben was too ill to join us on our Scotch tour as planned. My sister and Harvey and I and several friends had a lovely time in Scotland with Bachs tour. The next year Harvey and I went again on a tour of western Scotland, staying at Oban and visiting Iona. It was all so lovely.

Changes... for the worse

In 1962 it was the half century celebrations of the Tiddy Hall. Those of us who still remembered Mr. Tiddy with affection and gratitude for the differ-ence he had made to our lives, had looked forward for years to having a real get-together with folk song and Morris dancing as he would have liked it. But the secretary and committee would not have it so, and when I dared to say it was an insult to his memory to have a Bingo-and-twist sort of celebrations, I was more or less ostracised for quite a time. But I don't think I shall ever forgive them for what was said and done.

Then I had some Honeybone cousins from New Zealand call. His father had emigrated from Ascott when he was a child so they wanted to take pictures of the Church and family graves. I was heartbroken to find that the Vicar and Churchwardens had destroyed all the graves of my mother's family like a row of antheaps, despite all the protests I had made at previous meetings. I had tended these graves all my life. It is a wicked heartless thing that strangers should come here and destroy families who have lived here for centuries. I wrote to the Bishop and asked him why the Church was committing suicide here. I said, 'They have taken our Vicar, sold our Vicarage, broken up the choir and ringers etc., now they are destroying our ancient Churchyard'. But all I got back was a page of utter piffle! No help or reason. Then I had a terrific row in the Churchyard with the Vicar – he was most insulting to me and really beastly, so I've not been able to make myself go to Church since. So after a life-time of working for the Church and the Hall, and for the good of the village, this is the thanks one gets. Such is life!

There are so many things Ascott had when I was a child and has now lost in so-called progress. To mention a few things: the Vicarage, with a resident Vicar and family, the sexton, carpenter and undertaker, midwife, blacksmith, shoemaker, choir, ringers, sports teams, W.E.A., folk dance club, etc. etc. Soon the railway too. Anyway, we were lucky to have had such a happy life between the wars.

Two years ago I went on a tour of Cornwall, this year I went to Scotland again. My husband's father died last year at the age of 84. His mother was 88 last week. Harvey will soon be 19 and is completely engrossed in car rally driving. Each year seems to go quicker than the last one.

Your final question – what advice would I give to my grandchild? I think I would say this:

Don't ever have or do things to be the same as everyone else, but to be different. It's much more satisfying, and more fun. And don't wait until you are over 40 to have your first child – it's a hard and difficult thing to face in so many ways.

But I don't suppose they would take the slightest notice of anything I said!

Winning first prize

We were invited to attend a meeting at Rhodes House, Oxford for the presentation of the Awards won in this County Competition. My sister went with me, it reminded us of the days when we used to go to Rhodes House to the W.E.A. Summer Schools. There were eighty-eight competitors from all over Oxfordshire so I was absolutely surprised when I was called up as the First Prize winner.

The awards were presented by Lady Tweedsmuir, who said we were practically next door neighbours, as she lives at Burford. I felt specially thrilled as her husband, John Buchan, has always been my most favourite author.

Presenting a bouquet to Vanessa Redgrave

I also had another eventful day on 4th July, 1966, when I was invited to the opening of the T.U.L.C. History Exhibition at Congress House, London, to present the bouquet to Miss Vanessa Redgrave, the famous actress who was to open the Exhibition. My sister, and my neighbour Mrs. Powell, went with me and her son David met us, as they had both acted in the play *Over the Hills to Glory*. Everyone was so kind to us, we had a great time. We had lunch in the Dining Room below the Congress Hall. The Exhibition was arranged on tables and stands showing the records of the 200 years' struggle and history of the Labour movement in Britain. Many old newspapers, documents, pictures etc. told the stories of past struggles and trials.

The Ascott under Wychwood exhibit was on a stand with my plays and old posters of when we performed it in 1952 with mostly relatives and connections of the characters taking part. Pictures of Ascott I had taken of the actual spots that come into the story, and the most treasured article of our exhibition that had so pleased the Committee, because it seemed such a personal touch. This was a lovely old patchwork quilt that was made by one of the women who went to prison. As she had her baby with her she was excused

hard labour, and in the true Ascott habit she 'just got on with her sewing' and worked away at her patchwork quilt in prison. It was given me by Mrs. Pearl Moriss whose foster

Doris presents her bouquet to Vanessa Redgrave, 4 July 1966.

mother, Mrs. Ellen Beauchamp, was the daughter of Mrs. Smith who went to prison. I'm not sure if Mrs. Beachamp was the baby who went too but I think she was. So it was a proud moment for me to see 'The Ascott Women' standing side by side with the Tolpuddle Martyrs and to feel that at last they really had gone 'Over the Hills to Glory'.

I was rather bewildered to find myself on the dais with Miss Vanessa Redgrave and Mrs. Lena Jeger M.P. (two lovely, friendly persons), the Lord Mayor and Lady Mayoress, Mr. Walter Southgate who had collected most of the items, Mr. Henry Fry the Secretary, and several M.P.s etc. It was hoped that the Exhibition would tour the country in time.

As we found we were in the same road as the British Museum, we spent a while there to finish up a very happy day.

1968 was a hard year to live through.

In the New Year I had an illness which left me with bad eyesight and headaches. On March 12th Harvey married Linda Stephens at Charlbury Church, it was a lovely wedding and nice to have a family gathering. So he left home and went to live at Charlbury. On Sunday, 9th June, my mother-in-law passed peacefully away at College Farm. She was 92. On Monday 10th June, my sister died suddenly with thrombosis. On Wednesday Grandma was cremated at Oxford. On Friday Florence's funeral was at Kidlington Church. The Church and Churchyard were full of people, so many knew and loved her. They have made a 'Florence Memorial' cupboard in the vestry to hold the lovely vestments and tapestries she made.

In 1969 they have destroyed and burned down Ascott Station. It was built about 1855.

Now College Farm is to be sold and we hope to attain the state of 'peaceful retirement' at last.